Devotions to Strengthen Your Walk with God

Proverbs FOR BUSY Women

Edited by Mary C. Busha

*Contributors include Barbara Johnson
and Evelyn Christenson*

BROADMAN
& HOLMAN
PUBLISHERS

Nashville, Tennessee

4253-86
0-8054-5386-5

Dewey Decimal Classification: 242.643
Subject Heading: Devotional Literature \ Woman—Religious Life \
Bible. O.T. Proverbs
Library of Congress Card Catalog Number: 94-36448

Interior design by Leslie Joslin
Cover design by The Puckett Group

Library of Congress Cataloging-in-Publication Data
Proverbs for busy women / Mary Busha, editor.
    p.   cm.
Contents: 1. Devotions to refresh you in your work — 2. Devotions to build up your relationships — 3. Devotions to strengthen your walk with God.
ISBN 0-8054-5386-5
1. Bible. O.T. Proverbs—Meditations. 2. Women—Prayer-books and devotions—English. 3. Christian life. I. Busha, Mary Catherine, 1945–.
    BS1465.4.P76   1995
    242'.643—dc20   94-36448
                                                               CIP

This book in the series
is dedicated
to my precious Lord and Savior,
Jesus Christ,
who so lovingly redeemed me
and shed His grace upon me.

May the words of my mouth
and the meditations of my heart
be acceptable in Your sight.

ACKNOWLEDGMENTS

Mary C. Busha

Many thanks to each woman who has written for this book. You are unique in the kingdom of God, and, because of that, He has worked uniquely in you. Thank you for sharing from your life with those who will read this book.

A special thanks, too, to Janis Whipple, editor at Broadman & Holman, for believing in this project and to Broadman & Holman Publishers for allowing this dream to continue.

As always, many thanks to my husband, Bob, for his special kind of love and encouragement.

CONTENTS

INTRODUCTION

Each one of us is unique. Isn't that wonderful! When God created His children, He did not roll us out on a heavenly cutting board and use a cookie cutter to mold each one of us.

No, when He knit us together in our mothers' wombs, He gave each of us our own peculiar personalities, special character traits, unique physical features, and a variety of gifts and talents.

And so it is with our relationship to the Lord. While He loves us equally, because He is no respecter of persons, He is intimately involved in a special way with each one of us.

As you read about the intimate workings of our heavenly Father in the lives of our contributing writers, we pray you will be inspired and encouraged to search the Scriptures and apply them to your own everyday experiences. Then be watchful for His unique messages to you, His special creation.

MY SOUL
LIMP

Barbara Anderson

For the LORD gives wisdom, and from his mouth
come knowledge and understanding.
Proverbs 2:6

Not long ago I sat with my daughter in the office of a specialist in orthopedic cancer. She had undergone biopsy surgery just two weeks before. That day we were to hear the results.

With misery in our hearts, we listened to his words. It seemed her leg must be amputated as soon as possible to keep the malignancy from spreading. My daughter cried while her four-year-old son bludgeoned the doctor with his little fists for "making Mommy cry." I sat in shock, unable to stop him or comfort my daughter. The diagnosis was devastating.

In the days that followed, I could not seem to find the inner strength I should have had as a Christian. My prayers were full of sobbing protests and petitions for my daughter's healing. As the two terrible weeks of waiting for the surgery passed, I finally began to realize that God was in control of this situation in which my hands were tied. He really did love my daughter, and His concern for her was even greater than

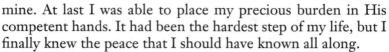

mine. At last I was able to place my precious burden in His competent hands. It had been the hardest step of my life, but I finally knew the peace that I should have known all along.

The day for the surgery came and went with successful results. Today my daughter is as beautiful as ever. She wears a prosthesis and has only a slight limp. Handicapped? Never! There are very few things she can't do, and her attitude is wonderful.

While passing through this terribly difficult time, I discovered that I was the one with the dreadful limp. Mine was a soul limp! What a lack of wisdom and faith I had shown. God had graciously used those painful weeks to show me a vacant area in my mind, an area containing knowledge but lacking in that strong faith which comes from true wisdom. I realized that waiting on God was not just words but an all-encompassing way of life.

Unfortunately, my soul limp stays with me. I encounter it whenever there is another test, another trial. It reminds me of my own human weakness; it also reminds me of the longsuffering and mercy my wonderful Savior extends to me as He controls each situation of my life—despite my dreadful soul limp.

Father, grant me the knowledge to see You in
all the circumstances of life, and the wisdom
to understand Your direction as I walk
in faith with You.
Amen.

❧

REGRETS ONLY

Niki Anderson

He who conceals his transgressions will
not prosper, but he who confesses and
forsakes them will obtain mercy.
Proverbs 28:13, RSV

Another birthday party. The familiar shape of the colored envelope addressed to my son hinted of its contents.

Eleven-year-old boys do not receive many other types of mail. I cued myself, "I mustn't forget to ask J.J. the date and time of the party so I can mark it on the calendar."

A few days later I asked, "When is the birthday party you were invited to? Be sure to give me the details so we can buy a gift on time." With engaging sincerity he answered me.

"Oh, don't worry, Mom. I don't have to take a present."

Well, this was a switch. No gift for a little boy's birthday party? I was curious.

"What do you mean no present?"

With kid-like candor he replied, "The invitation said regrets only!"

Regrets only. It was clear. J.J. did not understand the meaning of a social regret, but the implication was plain to him:

Regrets only must mean no gifts—a very reasonable conclusion for a boy not versed in closures such as RSVP, No Host Lunch, or Regrets Only.

Several days later, I was contemplating the grace of God. My contemplation stemmed from my strong sense of need. Little failures in many areas had left me with frequent pangs of regret. While particularly guilt-ridden one day, I heard J.J.'s words echo in my heart like an oracle from God. "Regrets only, child; that's all I require," God whispered in paraphrase.

Indeed, God does not call us to grovel in our mistakes. A little regret, biblically described as repentance, and we can move forward.

What a gift—this magnanimous forgiveness always flowing from God. Speaking of parties! Everyone is invited—little and big kids alike. And God is the gift bringer. We need come with regrets only.

> *Thank You, Lord, for Your invitation to for-*
> *giveness. Help me refrain from lingering in*
> *unnecessary guilt when You have provided,*
> *through Jesus' substitutionary death, the*
> *marvelous remedy for my sins.*
> *Amen.*

BUGS

Betty L. Arthurs

The wise woman builds her house, but with her own hands the foolish one tears hers down.
Proverbs 14:1

I touched the brown crumbs on my kitchen counter. So many times I had mindlessly wiped them up with my dishcloth; but this time I wondered, *Where are these coming from?* I looked up.

"John," I yelled to my husband, "come look!" A white, ant-like bug hung out of a hole in the corner of our ceiling. Speechlessly, we watched it greedily chew on our kitchen. Our twenty-five-year-old, newly purchased home had termites!

Horrified, we called an exterminator. He promised quick treatment, but it took four long sessions of drilling holes in the foundation of our house and around all the drain pipes. Then he pumped in a lethal pesticide, and finally the gnawing insects were gone. We felt fortunate so little damage had been done.

I thought of how often I allow little "bugs" to move quietly into my life. Before long they have eaten away at the peace in

7

my heart and then in my home. A small misunderstanding develops into a full-blown offense against one of my children. My unchecked resentment toward my husband's long work hours builds until there's a wall between us. One day I nurse a bad attitude toward all my homemaker responsibilities, and before long my opportunity is gone to serve my family unselfishly.

I must learn to be a ruthless exterminator. Daily Bible reading, personal worship time, and prayer are all powerful antidotes against the bugs in my life. When I read the Word, God's searchlight finds the flaws and cracks in my spiritual foundation. He lovingly exposes the real me and helps me change.

In personal praise time, I thank the Lord for all He has done for me. As I lift my hands in worship, I give my life to Him and can feel His peace surrounding my home. Prayer allows me to share with Jesus all my needs, knowing He cares for and loves me. His unchanging love is the most potent "pesticide" against "termites" trying to destroy my family and me.

Lord, thank You for exposing the "bugs" in my
heart and helping me become a wise woman.
Amen.

YOU MUST CHOOSE

Leslie B. Bagg

Blessed is the man who always fears the LORD,
but he who hardens his heart falls into trouble.
Proverbs 28:14

My friend Carol was angry with me.

"Why do you always say, 'Well, what do you think the Lord wants you to do? Why don't you pray about it?' I don't want to pray about it. I want to do something that will get me out of this situation. Besides, I've seen you crumble under pressure lots of times!"

That final remark left me speechless. Carol was right. I had failed to follow my own advice many times in the past. Her words haunted me the rest of the day. I finally decided to write her a letter.

Dear Carol,

When I accepted Jesus as my Savior and Lord, I decided to seek His will in my life and to obey it. His Holy Spirit living in me gives me the power to do that.

However, I do have a choice in the matter. I can obey and do what He wants me to do, or I can disobey and do what I want to do. The choice is up to me. That's the hard part.

When I pray for guidance and help in hard situations, that usually doesn't get me out of them. God uses those times to grow, teach, and bless me. He grows me to make me become more like Jesus—to develop His character traits. He teaches me that I can endure tough situations and learn things I might never have learned if I hadn't gone through them. He blesses me because His Holy Spirit in me gives me the power to do the hard but right thing when needed. When I'm obedient, God gives His peace "which transcends all understanding." I've experienced that peace many times (remember when my dad died and my mom was sick?). I regret that you've probably seen more of the crumbling-under-pressure times.

The point is this: I can choose to follow the Lord's will and be blessed, or follow my own desires and end up in trouble. When God takes me through the situation and grows, teaches, and blesses me, I'm so thankful afterward that I've obeyed, and I wonder, *Why don't I do that all the time?* But if I could, then I wouldn't need a Savior, would I?

Love,
Your Friend

Dear Lord, in tough times, help me to choose
Your will and not mine. Thank You for Your
Holy Spirit living in me who gives me the
power to obey You.
Amen.

BEAUTIFUL TAPESTRY

Victoria J. Bastedo

A man's steps are directed by the LORD.
How then can anyone understand his own way?
Proverbs 20:24

One day I decided to try my hand at cross-stitch. I had never done anything like it before, so my two little girls, Meribeth and Amber, were curious. Amber, the baby, had contented herself with taking my carefully separated thread lengths and pulling them all out. Two-year-old Meribeth wanted to explore all of the options.

"No, Meribeth," I said, "this is Mommy's."

"Look what you got!" she said, reaching for it.

"Yes, it's Mommy's sewing. Don't touch it!"

Carefully, we both leaned over my work, as I tried to push the needle up through the appropriate hole.

When I was able to finally poke the unseen needle up through the fabric, we were both triumphant.

As she saw the needle tip appearing, she shouted in my ear, "That's a bug!" Then, satisfied that she'd figured it out, she ran off to play. I laughed and went back to my stitching.

My handiwork reminds me of the threads of my life that, taken apart, seem to make no sense at all. Sometimes I even try to take the tapestry out of God's hands, uncaring of the mess I might make of things. Often, as I study His handiwork, I have no idea of what He is doing.

I'm reminded also of all the times I've interrupted God in His efforts to weave the threads of my life. Patiently He endures my meddling, even allowing me to play with the threads. But, I'm thankful that He controls the needle. He keeps the tapestry firmly in His hands as He weaves my life into the lives of others. I'm comforted as I realize that I can rely on Him to make my life something beautiful.

Dear Lord, thank You for loving me enough to keep control of my life. Help me to remember to trust You and realize that You are making my life a beautiful tapestry.
Amen.

OBSCENE OR OPPORTUNE?

Faye L. Braley

Do not enter the path of the wicked,
and do not proceed in the way of evil men.
Proverbs 4:14, NASB

The telephone rang as I was in the middle of dinner preparations. Musing on the certainty of telephone calls when you have dough on your hands, I went to answer it. My vexation increased when I heard the obscenities which were coming over the line.

I have heard (and tried) many suggestions for handling such unwelcome calls. This time I quietly laid the receiver down and went about my dinner preparations. I made sure the pots and pans rattled and the cupboard doors banged, and I sang snatches of songs from the music our choir was learning.

After a bit, I heard the electronic signal from the telephone, warning me the party on the line had hung up and my receiver was off the hook. As I returned the receiver to the cradle, I couldn't help wondering if the caller had heard any of the sounds from my kitchen. Perhaps he wasn't listening, only venting whatever demon had possession of his mind.

Later on, as I reflected on the depravity of that call, the Holy Spirit gently brought conviction to my heart. I began to examine my conscience for double standards. Though I had refused to listen to an obscene call, was I always as careful to shut out other obscenities from my life? What about the television programs I watch, the books and magazines I read? How many times have I shrugged off the uncomfortable feeling caused by questionable content and finished the program or the book?

In a way, I am grateful to that unknown caller. Oh, I don't in any way appreciate his message, but I do appreciate the springboard it provided for God's intervention into my own habits. Although it is something that needs daily vigilance, I have learned to be more discriminating in my choices of viewing or reading. Thank God for the obscene telephone call.

Thank You, Lord, for Your Holy Spirit, and for
His readiness to convict and correct. Help me
to stay sensitive to His voice.
Amen.

DID YOU THINK TO PRAY?

Irene B. Brand

A gentle answer turns away wrath,
but a harsh word stirs up anger.
Proverbs 15:1

I'd driven over fifty miles and had taken thirty minutes to find a parking place. When I arrived at the conference room, I learned that the writers' meeting had been rescheduled. Seething with indignation, I tried to contact Jerry, the president of the organization, who hadn't notified me of the change. He was out of his office.

Angrily, I started home, driving at the maximum speed, venting my abused feelings on the automobile. I'm sure God was saying, "Calm down," but He couldn't get my attention.

I turned on the tape player. My hands slowly relaxed on the steering wheel, and I eased my foot on the accelerator when the words of a gospel song spoke to my rebellious thoughts, reminding me of the importance of prayer when my heart was full of anger.

When I finally got the message, did I pray? No, I laughed—laughed at myself for allowing a minor incident to sour my

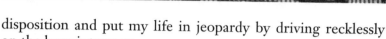

disposition and put my life in jeopardy by driving recklessly on the busy interstate.

But I shuddered when I thought of the greatest danger I'd avoided. Membership in that organization gave me an opportunity for Christian witnessing in the secular world, and I'd nearly muffed it. If I had been successful in contacting Jerry, I would have given him a tongue-lashing because he hadn't notified me about the meeting change.

The song's message caused me to take an appraising, inward look. Wasn't my intolerance toward the shortcomings of others worse than Jerry's forgetfulness? I prayed for God to forgive me and grant me a change of attitude.

While He still had my attention, God spoke through His Word, "Be kind and compassionate to one another, forgiving each other, just as in Christ God forgave you" (Eph. 4:32).

How thankful I was that God had reminded me through music and His Word that I wasn't perfect either. When Jerry telephoned his apology, I assured him, "I've already forgiven you."

Whether my forgiving spirit made any difference in Jerry's spiritual values, I may never know; but harsh words from me wouldn't have pointed him toward my Savior nor to the importance of living a Christian life.

Father, may I forgive others as You've forgiven

me. Help me to answer gently when

I've been wronged.

Amen.

TRUST ME

Shirley Brosius

Trust in the LORD with all your heart
and lean not on your own understanding.
Proverbs 3:5

As a new Christian, Proverbs 3:5 was the first verse I memorized. Little did I know that five years later I would cling to it as a lifeline.

Excited about having a baby brother or sister for our two sons, I embarked on my third pregnancy in high spirits. A fear of childbirth had plagued me, but it evaporated in my prayers. Even when my doctor ordered bed rest because of premature contractions, I was at peace. Wasn't my whole church family praying for us? Surely, all would be well.

Our beautiful baby daughter, Christy Marie, was born early on an April Fools' Day morning. But two hours later she turned around and ran back into the open arms of her Lord. My husband and I were heartbroken. I felt that God had played a cruel April Fools' joke on us. Babies don't just die in this day and age! What had gone wrong? Why had God let us down?

In those first days of fresh grief, the pages of Scripture seemed lifeless and dry. I clung to Proverbs 3:5. God had said, "Trust Me." That's what I wanted to do. In response to my questions, my pastor patiently explained that we can ask God's favor, but we cannot demand it. God is sovereign and certainly capable of intervening in the natural course of events, but He is not obligated to us to do so.

Ever so gradually I came to accept the fact that we live in an imperfect world subject to germs and physical limitations. Our loving heavenly Father does not always remove these obstacles from our path, but He is pleased to walk through them with us. By such a demonstration of His grace, His glory can be seen as surely as in a miraculous healing. At such times we do not need to "understand," but we do need to trust Him. As we do, He leads us on in the path of life step by step.

> *Lord, in difficult times help me to keep my*
> *eyes on You, trusting You to walk*
> *through them with me.*
> *Amen.*

CONFIDENCE THROUGH THE STORM

Karen Carncross

For the LORD will be your confidence and will
keep your foot from being caught.
Proverbs 3:26, RSV

The snowstorm hit—it was impossible for me get home. I had nowhere to lay my head. I had never experienced this before.

I'd had an early afternoon doctor's appointment in Bellevue, which I needed to keep. I thought I could make it there and back with no trouble, but I had tire chains just in case. After a two-hour wait at the doctor's office, the snow was heavier than I had anticipated. A considerate young couple helped me put the chains on, and I headed for the Evergreen Point Bridge.

Six miles and six hours later, I reached the bridge, only to find it closed. I stopped at three motels. There was no room anywhere. (This was the week before Christmas; in my most forlorn moment I felt like asking if anyone had a stable where I could spend the night.) By now it was midnight. I had been praying all along and had felt God's presence with me, but now I was desperate. I said, "Lord, I don't know where to go. I'm totally dependent on You."

I started driving again, then noticed a sign to downtown Seattle via Mercer Island. I made it across the bridge, and then I heard a loud clanging and realized a tire chain had broken. I turned off the freeway and then the car started swirling. I hung on to the steering wheel—and to Jesus—and somehow the car stopped before I hit the intersection traffic.

People stepped forward to help. Two men pushed the car out of harm's way and two young couples offered to walk with me up the hill to a nearby hotel, where again there was no room. But this time I was offered the use of a small lobby couch, a blanket and pillow, and a cup of hot apple cider.

I didn't sleep much—bright lights, busy sounds, and Christmas music kept penetrating my exhaustion. But I rested deeply in the Lord; I felt cared for and safe.

This experience taught me that God may not alter natural occurrences when we pray for help, yet somehow Jesus stands between me and my fear. I had felt the comfort of His Spirit and assurance of His Word, even when I was crying and telling Him how scared I felt.

His grace is greater than circumstances, stronger than emotions. I learned in the midst of the storm, He will be my confidence and will keep my foot from being caught.

Lord, Your presence gives me the confidence to
keep going through the storm. Your
faithfulness is greater than my fears,
and for this I praise You.
Amen.

GOD'S IN THE LIFE-CHANGING BUSINESS!

Annie Chapman

Happy is the man who finds wisdom, and the man who gets understanding, for the gain from it is better than gain from silver and its profit better than gold.
Proverbs 3:13–14, RSV

In the spring of 1988 I was asked to speak at a ladies' retreat for the Southeast Christian Church in Louisville, Kentucky, scheduled for the following March. My husband, Steve, and I had been to the church before, so the people were familiar with me and my message.

While praying about what I should prepare to share (I was to deliver four one-hour presentations), I felt the Lord impress on me to share how He could change the things we hate most about ourselves. As I contemplated this subject matter, I argued with the Lord.

"Lord, I can't speak on that subject because I have never let You deal with the things that keep me back. I am unqualified."

I sensed His reply, "Well, we have a year to do that." I thought about Esther and how she was put on a twelve-month beauty regimen (see Esth. 2:12). So for the following twelve months I made a list of the things about myself that bothered me and thus limited the message of my life. I set out, with God's help, to change these things. There were many things in my life that could not be seen that needed changing. For instance, I watched too much television. I needed to be more consistent in my prayer life and Bible study. There was necessary work concerning my relationship with my children, such as the angry responses to childish behavior. And there was the deep feelings of inferiority (self-loathing) that caused me to push people back, rejecting them before they could reject me.

These problems were biggies for me to work on. There were also some outward things that needed to change. I've always had a weight problem, and so there was the issue of thirty-five extra pounds that needed to come off. I wanted to remove some moles. In fact, my entire appearance needed revamping since I hadn't changed my hair style in twenty years.

Well, 1988 became a life-changing year for me. When I arrived to share that weekend in 1989, I walked in and no one recognized me. The year before they saw a size fourteen plus, matronly woman; but the woman who showed up to speak a year later was a size six, confident person who knew that God could change a life.

Thank You, Father, that You're in the life-changing business, and that nothing is too difficult for You to accomplish in my life. May the changes You've brought in me give testimony to Your goodness and mercy and ability to change Your children inside and out.

Amen.

FOOLS RUSH IN

Jeri Chrysong

*Also it is not good for a person to be without
knowledge, and he who makes
haste with his feet errs.*
Proverbs 19:2, NASB

I like to think I still have some kid in me. This attitude was the motivating factor in playing my sons' game while walking on the beach. Lucas and Sammy, ages nine and six, play this game frequently. It's called "Using Mommy's Footsteps."

The object of their game is to reuse my empty footprints in the sand and whoever can (1) get their foot into my discarded footprints first, or (2) knock the other guy off balance or off my trail, wins. For them the game is fraught with hilarity. As for myself, the jury is still out on my enjoyment level, as it depends on how many times my Achilles' heel is trounced while the game is played. Anyway, alone one afternoon, I found myself playing the spin-off, "Using Someone Else's Footsteps."

Possessing rather large feet for a woman, I found it difficult to find footprints my feet would fit into, but eventually I found a usable trail. Because the sand was compact, slippage

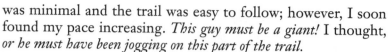

was minimal and the trail was easy to follow; however, I soon found my pace increasing. *This guy must be a giant!* I thought, *or he must have been jogging on this part of the trail.*

In order to keep up with his longer stride, I began hopping from footprint to footprint. My pace increased radically from the gentle moseying of my earlier walk, and several times I lost my balance and landed on my backside in the sand. I looked and felt foolish, and I didn't enjoy the game anymore. How difficult it was to follow in someone else's footsteps.

Proverbs 19:2 states that "He who makes haste with his feet errs." Trying to keep up with another's walk is unnatural. God created me a unique individual, not someone's carbon copy. Besides, He would rather I follow Him.

How much more enjoyable my life's walk is when I stick to my own pace, my own stride, and place my footsteps in His.

*Father, let me not rush. Let me always be con-
tent with Your pace. And let my feet always
travel in the direction You would have me go.
Amen.*

FREE TO WALK WITH HIM

Linda Clare

Free yourself, like a gazelle from the hand of the hunter, like a bird from the snare of the fowler.
Proverbs 6:5

Worry had taken me prisoner. I fretted about everything from furniture to finances. If my husband was late getting home, I imagined a hideous car crash. If I planned a picnic, I worried about the weather. I spent many hours as chief worrier for my four children.

One of my duties as Worrymom was to remind my youngest to keep her shoes and socks on when playing outside. Even though the doctor said colds come from germs, I feared the cool, damp climate where we live would make her sick.

One rainy afternoon, I found her mud-caked Mary Janes and soaked anklets lying deserted on the front porch. My four-year-old daughter skipped across the flooded lawn, kicking up free feet like a preschool gazelle.

Confronting my fugitive from patent leather, I pointed to the soggy jumble. Didn't she know she could come down with something?

She wiggled her toes and flashed her most adorable grin. "I'm sorry," she said. "It's just that my feet were in jail. Now they're free."

I looked down at my sneakers, laced up tight. Worry had pinched my faith like confining shoes, and I'd allowed it to keep me prisoner.

As I kicked off my shoes, I asked God to help free me from the snare of worry. My hair got drenched and the neighbors stared, but my daughter and I played in the muddy yard. I wasn't worried, for I knew I was free to walk—or skip—with Him.

Lord, free me from worry. Help me to abandon

the cares that jail my heart.

Amen.

Stop, Look, and Listen!

Patti Townley Covert

"But he who listens to me shall live securely,
and shall be at ease from the dread of evil."
Proverbs 1:33, NASB

A vibration silently shook the steel rail beneath my foot. I stepped back and wondered if a train was coming.

After a hot day on the beach, my six-year-old son and I were in a hurry to get home. Taking a shortcut meant crossing tracks where there was no barrier. "Whoooo, whoooo"—a train whistle sounded softly from around the bend.

"Listen, Mom, there's a train coming," B.J. tugged at me. "Hurry!" he hollered, wanting to beat it across the tracks.

"Let's wait," I said, gripping his arm firmly.

Some teenaged boys laughed and yelled, "Come on, chicken!" as they raced the approaching danger. My heart ached as I remembered Mike, my old high school buddy who raced a train and lost. "Chugga, chugga, whooo, whooo!" I continued to hold B.J. securely.

Sometimes, just like B.J., I want to race the trains of life. Warning whistles of sin or evil blow deep inside my mind. It's

tempting to ignore them as society laughs and yells, "C'mon, if it feels good, do it."

Danger approaches from around bends where I can't see. Yet the thrill of racing to accomplish my goals tempts me to ignore warnings and become oblivious to consequences. I tug at my heavenly Father and holler, "C'mon, let's go!"

But His Word grips me and pulls me back. Stopping long enough to pray and study the Bible isn't easy; but, when I do, it helps set my priorities straight and keeps them that way. Knowing God and His promises helps me stay in the safety of His hand.

Looking through my Father's eyes gives me eternal perspective. He can see around those bends. He knows exactly what the future holds and gives me the wisdom I need to make good, long-term choices.

Listening for and obeying my Father's voice helps prevent me from making bad decisions. I live secure in the knowledge that if I stop, look, and listen, I'll never get run over by a train.

Father God, please help me take time for You.

Open my eyes to see You, my ears to hear You,

and enable me to obey Your voice.

Amen.

THE
MIRACLE OF
WOMANHOOD

Betty Edwards

He hears the prayer of the righteous.
Proverbs 15:29, RSV

As I reflect over the years, I can't help but feel a great appreciation for the pleasure of being created a woman and all that goes with it, even when it comes to my monthly cycle. I've heard some women refer to it as a curse. To me it's more of an honor.

One summer, as a young teen, I attended a youth camp. I couldn't believe it one afternoon as I sat in the old outhouse to discover that my monthly period had begun. I was horrified. I'd had my first period a few years previously; but because of not having one since that time, this had come as a complete shock, especially since I wasn't prepared. What would I do? I had no provision, and in those days you just didn't discuss personal things openly.

Suddenly I remembered part of a sermon the evangelist had preached the evening before. All I could remember hearing was, "When you're in a crisis and you don't know what to do,

when you're afraid and at the end of your rope, just let go, and Jesus will catch you."

As I closed my eyes to pray, I could picture myself hanging on to one thin thread at the end of a very frayed rope. Then mentally I let go.

I left the outhouse and started back for the girls' camp. About halfway up the path, the pastor's wife came out the back door of the old farmhouse nearby. She called to me, then quietly said, "Betty, if you or any of the girls need any sanitary napkins or anything personal like that, just go up the back stairway to the bedroom on the left. In the top right-hand dresser drawer, you'll find everything you need."

That was the night I dedicated my life to God, because for the first time I realized just how personally He knew me and cared about me. Since then I have never looked upon the miracle of being a woman and all it entails as being a burden.

Now as I near the end of menopause, I'm excited for the season of life that comes next. What a privilege to have been created and chosen by God to experience the miracle of womanhood. To know that the egg that was miraculously brought forth each month, through no effort or knowledge of my own, could bring forth another human being. From this body of mine, God has allowed three wonderful children to be born. And now I have eight beautiful grandchildren.

Thank You, Lord, for creating me to be a
woman, mother, and grandmother. May my
life bring glory to You as You continue to carry
out the plan You have for my life.
Amen.

PURSUING A DISCIPLINED LIFE

Elisabeth Elliot

He who refuses correction is his own worst
enemy, but he who listens to
reproof learns sense.
Proverbs 15:32, NEB

A renewed mind has an utterly changed conception, not only of reality but of possibility. A turn away from the kingdom of this world to the kingdom of God provides a whole set of values based not on the human word, but on Christ's. Impossibilities become possibilities.

One of my husband's greatest gifts is friendliness. He meets people easily and quickly puts them at ease. I don't. He helps me by his example, and I am learning; but I also need his word. Recently he spoke to me about not having been as friendly as I should have been to a stranger. My immediate response to his remark was anger.

That particular stranger happened to be a young person who stopped me in a hotel and addressed me by a nickname used only by my family and old friends. My annoyance showed, Lars said, in spite of my having smiled, greeted her, and expressed an interest in what she was doing. Lars gave me

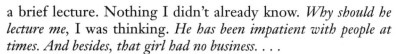

a brief lecture. Nothing I didn't already know. *Why should he lecture me*, I was thinking. *He has been impatient with people at times. And besides, that girl had no business. . . .*

My reaction was "real"; that is, it certainly was what came to mind first. I didn't speak what I was thinking, but my thoughts were in the old pattern—not the new, not the mind of Christ. "Reality" is often evil. I knew my thoughts toward this girl were wrong to begin with. The Holy Spirit reminded me of the truth: Let God remold your mind. Set your mind on heavenly things.

Think Christ was the new thought that came. Where did it come from? Not from me. Not from a secular mind-set. The Holy Spirit reminded—re-minded—me. "He who refuses correction is his own worst enemy, but he who listens to reproof learns sense" (Prov. 15:32).

"Lord, help me to face the truth of what Lars is saying to me, instead of blocking it out by self-defense," I prayed. I have found it necessary, sometimes deliberately, to refuse thoughts of what someone has done and ask for help to dwell on what Christ has done for that person and wants to do for him and for me.

The disciple who honestly seeks to let God remold her mind will direct her energies to a total surrender of obedient love. With her heart open to the Spirit of God, she will be in a position to learn wisdom.

> *Heavenly Father, thank You for reminding me*
> *to "think Christ" when I'm tempted to harbor*
> *wrong thoughts toward others. Help me daily*
> *to set my mind on heavenly things.*
> *Amen.*

CONFIDENCE IN AN EMERGENCY

Remi Adeeko Enobakhare

The LORD will be your confidence.
Proverbs 3:26, NKJV

Anyone who has ever had small children will bear witness: Kids move quickly!

Once, when my son Joshua was only ten months old, he was playing with a porcelain cup that I didn't even know was near him. Before I knew it he broke the mug, fell on it, and cut himself, producing a gash beneath his little finger that would require six stitches. Just looking at the little bleeding hand made me want to burst into tears, but I had to administer first aid and get help.

Later, in the emergency room of the hospital, doctors and nurses seemed to loll around and didn't even look at little Joshua's finger for over an hour. After complaining and pleading to one staff member after another, I finally did what I should have done in the first place, I cried out to God.

"Lord, I've been putting all of my confidence in people who don't love my son or consider him a priority. Father, You love him even more than I; he belongs to You. You made his hand, and You can heal it. Let these people hurry and get to him, and meanwhile let him not be in pain."

Joshua immediately began to nurse and soon fell asleep, so I knew he was no longer hurting. Shortly thereafter both a doctor and a nurse attended to him and carefully sewed him up, as his father and distraught mother talked to and distracted him from the ongoing procedure. My active little boy was bandaged up with lots of padding and, with the doctor's blessing, sent home. The next day he was crawling all over the house again.

I believe that those dear to us benefit from the relationship that we cultivate with the Lord. When I asked Him to help my Joshie, He certainly came through for me, just as He always has when I've called out to Him. I just had to remember in whom I need to place my confidence.

Father, help me to remember that You are my

confidence in every situation and will

always prove Yourself faithful.

Amen.

RESPONDING IN LOVE

Marjorie K. Evans

*He that hath pity upon the poor lendeth
unto the Lord; and that which he hath
given will he pay him again.*
Proverbs 19:17, KJV

One day I was busy working on a devotional article about God's love. Suddenly, the ringing of the telephone interrupted my thoughts.

Oh, dear, who can that be? I wondered. *I really need to finish this article so I can read it to the critique group tomorrow and then mail it out.*

The caller was a worker from a local rehabilitation center asking if I had any good used clothing or household items that I could have ready for them the next day. She went on to say they were in dire need of clothing. I explained that I was too busy to sort over anything that day. She graciously replied, "I understand. I'll call again."

So I went back to my writing, but ideas refused to come. Suddenly I was conscience-stricken as I thought of Jesus' teaching in Matthew: "'Lord, when did we see you hungry and feed you, or thirsty and give you something to drink?

35

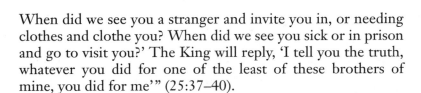

When did we see you a stranger and invite you in, or needing clothes and clothe you? When did we see you sick or in prison and go to visit you?' The King will reply, 'I tell you the truth, whatever you did for one of the least of these brothers of mine, you did for me'" (25:37–40).

Full of remorse, I thought, *How can I write an article about God's love when my life doesn't exhibit love toward those who need help?*

"Forgive me, dear Lord," I prayed in deep repentance. Then I called the rehabilitation center and told them I would have a box ready for their truck the next day.

Peace came as I took time out from writing to fill a large container with clothes. And with the peace came new ideas for the article.

Dear heavenly Father, touch my heart with
Your compassion so that I will always
respond in love to
those less fortunate than I.
Amen.

LAND TO WORK, NOT FANTASY

Kira Love Flores

He who works his land will have abundant food,
but he who chases fantasies lacks judgment.
Proverbs 12:11

As I finished reading another "happy ending" novel, I wondered why this world couldn't really be more like that. My world had seen and experienced too much pain and abuse. I preferred any other world but this! And that meant chasing fantasies.

My mind was so filled with daydreaming, and with novels and their happy endings, that I was trying constantly to squeeze reality to fit the castle in my sky. I wanted this world to be a better place, where trauma would end with joy in less than two hours. But this complex, fallen world cannot be contained within three hundred pages; and the wounds inflicted here leave scars that will remain until Christ returns and re-creates the world to be that place for which we long. But in the meantime, this world is it. *Despair.*

I wanted my husband to transcend ordinary life and become a hero from one of my novels. As wonderful as he is, he simply could not measure up. *Disappointment.*

I wanted my closest friends to be as faithful, perfect, and true as those in my daydreams; but, being human and at times unavailable, they could not meet my ideals. *Disillusionment.*

I wanted me to be a beautiful, infallible Christian woman, wife, mother, and friend—loved by everyone. But . . . well, you know, I'm not. *Dismay.*

Those four "D" words—despair, disappointment, disillusionment, and dismay—chased me into His Word for answers and into His presence for comfort.

The Lord showed me that as I accept what is and "work [my own] land" by planting, watering, nurturing, and pruning, then I "will have abundant food." In other words, as I get my hands dirty with reality, and enjoy the fruits of that reality (a husband who loves me, children who are healthy and typically rambunctious, friends whose motives are right, a Savior who has provided redemption in this sinful world and grace for all of my imperfections), I will be filled and I will be fulfilled.

Chasing fantasies reveals my lack of judgment; but as I work with the garden God has given me, I have wisdom, and my needs (not all my wishes, but my needs) are met.

Father, thank You for setting me free from
the bondage of escapism. May I choose Your
abundant life by accepting my humanity and
the life You've given me in this imperfect world.
Amen.

BEFORE I ASKED

Martha E. Garrett

A man's heart deviseth his way:
but the LORD directeth his steps.
Proverbs 16:9, KJV

Even though snow was falling, I knew I must continue looking for a house for my eight-year-old son and myself. Our apartment was ideal, except for one thing. The landlord (who lived below us) forgot to mention when we rented the apartment that a child was acceptable only if he didn't make any noise—such as walking and talking.

After spending hours driving up and down every street in our suburban town where I had lived for forty years and where I was sure I knew every house, I headed toward home, discouraged. Nothing was available in my price range. Then suddenly I stopped the car. There sat a house I had never seen before. Just the right size for two people, it was the perfect house for Sam and me. It was surrounded by trees to climb, and it had a fenced-in yard for a dog.

As I walked up the path to the front door, I prayed, "Lord, I know nothing is impossible for You. You promised to be a

Father to the widow and the orphan. Please make this house available even though there's no For Sale sign anywhere."

"Hi! Would you sell me your house?" I heard myself ask boldly when the door opened in reply to my knock.

The owner gasped. "You'll never believe this. Just today we received Air Force orders to report to the West Coast within two weeks. Please come in and meet my wife, and we'll discuss it with you."

When they mentioned the price, thousands of dollars less than I intended offering, I felt as though I could hang from the stars.

Everyone was pleased: the owners, Sam, and me.

Once again, I could joyfully share with my friends the wonderful care God takes of those who love Him!

Thank You, heavenly Father. You are
so merciful to Your children. Help me
to delight in being obedient to You.
In Jesus' precious name I approach
Your throne.
Amen.

ESPECIALLY FOR ME

Wilma Brown Giesser

*Trust in the LORD with all thine heart; and lean
not unto thine own understanding.*
Proverbs 3:5, KJV

At the age of eleven, I discovered something wonderful, something life-changing: I discovered that the Bible had something personal to say to me.

I desperately needed to know that. My world was crumbling. I had nothing tangible on which to hang. My father had been murdered a few months earlier, and the five of us children were being placed in a Masonic orphanage. Our young mother had neither the strength nor the resources to keep us at home. She had been forced to sell our two pet sheep and our pony. All of our new furniture had been given to relatives, and our house (the newest and finest in our small community) was being rented out.

We were standing in our empty living room; mother was giving Pastor Hill (our new renter and the new pastor in town) possession of our home. Unexpectedly, Pastor Hill gave me a Bible—the first one that I had ever owned. On the flyleaf

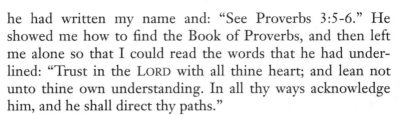

he had written my name and: "See Proverbs 3:5-6." He showed me how to find the Book of Proverbs, and then left me alone so that I could read the words that he had underlined: "Trust in the LORD with all thine heart; and lean not unto thine own understanding. In all thy ways acknowledge him, and he shall direct thy paths."

During the following months, I read and re-read those words: "Trust in the LORD." And I did. In fact, I learned to trust the LORD long before I knew enough to commit my life to Him.

Looking back, I now realize that these verses became my support system, my salvation. I had no trauma counseling, no bereavement counseling; but, with the faith of a child, I came to believe that these words were written especially for me.

My faith has stood the test of time. Or, better yet, God's Word has stood the test of time. True to His promises, He has directed my paths and in ways that have brought great joy and peace to me—even during times of heartache and pain.

I still feel, with childlike faith, that these verses were written especially for me—and for you.

Dear Lord, thank You that You personally
speak to each of us through Your Word, and
thank You for Pastor Hill, who cared enough
to share Your Word with a child.
Amen.

PRESERVING WISDOM

Sonya D. Gore

Get wisdom, get understanding: forget it not;
neither decline from the words of my mouth.
Forsake her not, and she shall preserve thee:
love her, and she shall keep thee.
Proverbs 4:5–6, KJV

Wouldn't it be nice if we could go to the department store and buy wisdom right off the shelf, or mix the proper ingredients and come up with the perfect recipe for it? Of course, if either of these were possible, the price would be beyond the reach of most people. I'm glad God chose to give preserving wisdom to all who seek Him.

From the beginning of time, wisdom has been demonstrated in the lives of godly women. Now some might argue the point when looking at Eve. Wisdom shined through, however, as Eve admitted her mistake, accepted the consequences, and then got up and went on.

Most of the time I have a little trouble admitting my mistakes. Just the other day I caught myself snapping at the kids. It wasn't anything out of the ordinary they were doing, just kid stuff—giggling, making messes, etc—until all of a sudden Mom turned into a green-eyed monster. Immediately a hush

fell over the room, and innocent faces stared up at me. In the silence, my mistake hit me head on. I was tired. I was frustrated. And I was taking it out on my children.

My prideful nature would have retreated to the bedroom to pout. Instead, preserving wisdom allowed me to admit my mistake and apologize. Soon the confusion disappeared, and the children were once again giggling and making messes.

The wisdom God gives for everyday life often goes unnoticed. All too often we look for wisdom in great and noble deeds. But the seemingly small ability to admit that we goofed is indeed a mighty demonstration of wisdom.

Thank You, Father, for showing me my mistakes. Help me to be the woman You want me to be. And fill me with Your preserving wisdom.
Amen.

MY FIRST PRIORITY IN LIFE

Ruth Bell Graham

The fear of the LORD leads to life;
and he who has it rests satisfied.
Proverbs 19:23, RSV

Our first priority in life is our relationship with God and nothing less.

Once on returning home from one of his many trips, my husband, Billy, brought the children a small puppet. It hung simply by strings from hooks supported by two nails on the end of a stick. The children had a wonderful time playing with it. Soon they brought it to me, a mass of tangled strings. To repair it, I had to hang it up by the hook to a nail in the fireplace mantel and slowly, patiently, painstakingly untangle the strings. So long as we kept the little puppet connected firmly to its overhead support, we were able to untangle it.

We are not puppets, but there is an interesting similarity. As long as we are firmly attached by our overhead support, we can remain that which we were created to be without becoming tangled. If we choose to put God first as He instructed in the Scriptures, our lives, like the puppet secured to the over-

head support, will remain untangled even though we are used to the limit by the master Puppeteer.

God is not only our Creator and Father; He is our reference point in both His written Word and His living Word, His Son and our Savior. In Him "we live and move and have our being." He is the beginning of life for us.

He is our Guide, Comforter, Corrector, Encourager, Companion. All through our lives on earth, He is our Father in heaven. He is all we ever lived for and had here on earth, or longed for and never knew. God will be in all our dreams and more. That we should allow Him to be in our lives is vital.

Heavenly Father, I choose this day and every day to make my relationship with You the first priority in my life. Thank You for being there for me. Thank You for being my overhead support!

Amen.

CONTROLLING
ANGRRRRR

Carlene Hacker

A fool gives full vent to his anger,
but a wise man keeps himself under control.
Proverbs 29:11

Without warning, his voice would build with intensity, his face would redden, his eyes would become daggers, until, like a volcanic eruption, my alcoholic father would spew his venomous hate and rage upon me. As a child, anger was an enemy that burned deep wounds into my soul.

As an adult, I lived with the agony of trying to avoid the anger of others and to stifle this terrifying, yet natural, emotion within me. I'd smile and pretend everything was fine. Then daily pressures would build, and I would explode . . . again. My husband and children knew the sudden outbursts all too well, which added guilt to remorse and growing hopelessness. No amount of prayer or Scripture reading helped. God was silent.

Then about three years ago, emotional pain drove me to see a Christian counselor and to attend meetings of Adult Children of Alcoholics. In my powerlessness, I prayed for the

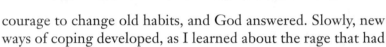

courage to change old habits, and God answered. Slowly, new ways of coping developed, as I learned about the rage that had once controlled me.

Writing poetry, journaling, taking part in physical exercise, and sharing with others became healthy tools to release and understand suppressed emotions. I became honest about feelings and the reasons for being angry. I saw anger not only as a cover but as a way of avoiding deeper pain. Anger hurt less than disappointment, shame, and worthlessness. In discovering truth, I was free to grieve and to forgive my family, myself, and God.

Instead of an enemy, anger became a signal that something was wrong and that God and I needed to talk. Rather than avoid uncomfortable situations, I took time to ask why I was angry, to identify hurt, and to use proper tools before confronting others. By facing, owning, and understanding emotions, I didn't need to suppress them. By stating my feelings, I didn't need to attack or blame. Instead, anger simply spurred healthy confrontation.

Not allowing anger and hurts to fester into volcanic reactions is a miracle that occurs one day at a time. I didn't think there was hope of ever keeping anger under control, but God is hope. Through Him anger has become my servant.

Thank You, God, that You have the

power to make enemies serve us,

and to make fools wise.

Amen.

A CHANGE OF HEART

Lynn Hallimore

It is not good to have zeal without knowledge,
nor to be hasty and miss the way.
Proverbs 19:2

I felt some uneasiness as I watched TV camera crews unload their equipment. Tonight's rally directed criticism at an existing authority, namely our school board and district supervisor. Excluded from their private session, our large group huddled outside the closed doors of their meeting place, placards in hand. We felt they had neglected to represent fairly our school.

Two squad cars arrived with deputy sheriffs. "Why are they here?" I asked the woman standing next to me. Her answer alarmed me.

"Someone said that the people serving on the board had received threats to their lives. The sheriffs are here to ensure their protection."

Groan. Why didn't I ask how this protest would be presented before I conceded to come? Of course, whoever had

threatened the board didn't necessarily belong to this group. It was probably some wacko.

One lady raised her fist in the air and began to chant as the film crews began their official roll. Others followed. I tried to shrink back. Another woman voiced jeers at the approaching board members.

That did it. I could not stay. Although I still felt the opposing stance was correct, I couldn't condone the manner in which the rally was being carried out.

Later that night I tried to analyze the evening's events and my involvement. But I didn't come to any conclusions until I read Proverbs 19:2, "It is not good to have zeal without knowledge." The opposition had snagged my emotions before my common sense told me to dig deeper and obtain all the facts I needed to make a responsible decision. "Nor to be hasty and miss the way." Although some causes prove worthy of support, the leaders in charge sometimes fail to extend the qualities of Christ. (I've seen this proven true in secular and religious circles.)

Next time, I will ask, "Why are you forming a protest? How will it be presented? Are you trying to annihilate your opponent or create in them a change of heart?"

Father, forgive me for my undisciplined
impulses. In my hurry, I ran past Your
directions for living. May I never again
endorse something that would
disgrace Your reign.
Amen.

AND THEN MY FATHER SPOKE

Freya Ottem Hanson

A word fitly spoken is like apples
of gold in a setting of silver.
Proverbs 25:11, RSV

I was home on break from college. I liked to discuss and debate with my father the new ideas I had heard in my college classes.

I talked about my religion class. "Now Jesus was a man; He burped like everyone else. He was just a man." My father listened intently, like a wise sage. He listened as I downplayed the divinity of Christ.

My father waited. I thought he might laugh or chime in with me, at least debate with me. This time he didn't. I began to wonder if I was getting through to him. Couldn't he handle some good, fun discussion? And then my father spoke. There was sadness in his voice. "Someday you will understand."

Understand! I was a college junior. I understood.

He continued, "Someday you will understand the sovereignty and power of God."

I was silenced. Instead of sadness, I now sensed a disgust in his voice as he brought the conversation to a close.

Someday I'll understand. I bristled inwardly with contempt as I headed for my bedroom.

My father and I didn't bring up the subject of the humanity of Christ again. I feared trampling on sacred ground. Yet the questions are still asked: Was Jesus just another man? Was He merely a fine teacher? Was He a prophet? Was He John the Baptist, Elijah, or Jeremiah? Or was He more?

I am no longer the college junior with all the answers. I am one who marks time in mid-life with more questions than answers. But there is one answer I must be prepared to give when Jesus asks me: "Who do you say that I am?" (Matt. 16:15).

Those college classes could reveal the humanity of Christ. But only God can reveal the true response. "You are the Christ, the Son of the living God" (Matt. 16:16).

Lord Jesus, let my words be like apples of gold

in a setting of silver declaring You the Mes-

siah, the holy One of God.

Amen.

A SOFT ANSWER

Dorothy M. Harpster

A gentle answer turns away wrath,
but a harsh word stirs up anger.
Proverbs 15:1

I remember an incident that happened when I was in third grade. The instructor in the little country school I attended was a busy person, teaching all of the classes for the eight grades every day.

There were few supplies. And the ones we had would have to last all year. One large package of construction paper had to be shared with five schools in the district.

I especially enjoyed art class. One day I was working diligently on a project when I accidently bumped the paste jar, sending it crashing to the floor. My joy quickly turned to fear as everyone now was staring at me. What would my teacher say?

Trembling, I went to explain to her that it was an accident and that I was sorry it had happened. To my surprise I didn't hear the harsh words I expected. Instead, she put her arms around my shoulders and walked with me back to my desk,

saying comforting things to me all the way. She said she was proud of me for telling the truth and for not blaming someone else for what I had done. When she saw the shattered glass, she helped me clean the floor. And then she encouraged me to begin my project again, which I did. I'll never forget that dear teacher.

Later when I became a teacher and taught for some forty-five years, I remembered her example. She taught me that gentle, kind words bring wonderful results.

Dear Father, help me always to remember
what You taught about gentleness,
forgiveness, and kindness. And
help me to practice them daily.
Amen.

MID-LIFE CRISIS

L. Jane Johnson

Keep my commands and you will live;
guard my teachings as the apple of your eye.
Bind them on your fingers;
write them on the tablet of your heart.
Proverbs 7:2–3

I was forty years old and having a mid-life crisis. I had been a Christian for twenty years and I was disappointed with God!

The disappointment had crept in slowly, first starting out as a certain type of boredom with life, in particular the life which God had given me. Nothing had turned out as I had thought it would. I was single and wished terribly to be married. The desire for children of my own left me with a seemingly unquenchable thirst and some resentment that my prayers had not been answered in the way that I had hoped.

Here I was, twenty years down the road of the Christian life, disappointed and wondering what, if anything, God had in store for me. My finances had taken an abrupt turnabout, leaving me with a somewhat more limited lifestyle than I was used to. Due to these circumstances, my life for some time had consisted of six-day work weeks in order to pay the bills. The affluent lifestyle I had enjoyed for so many years had

been curtailed. I was not without the necessities of life, it was true, but something for me had changed.

I remembered back to when I'd first become a Christian. Keeping the commands of God, as the proverb says, seemed to come naturally and joyfully for me. It was a privilege and a joy to write God's commands on my heart and try to live them out in the world.

I left college and the rat race began. Yes, I desired to follow Jesus, but surely God understood the necessity of being established in the world. If I was going to work for Him, I first needed to get my life together: the job, the car, the vacations, the house. Gradually, these things replaced the time and diligence with which I had searched the Scriptures.

Proverbs 7:2–3 stood as an invitation to return and to write the commands of God on my heart, to allow them, once again, to transform my life.

I found that my mid-life crisis called me out of the rush of a busy life and back to God. It called me away from the pleasures of the world, not wrong in themselves, but deadly, if in the pursuit of them I failed to find life.

Lord Jesus, help me to bind Your words on my fingers and write them on my heart, so that I will remember You and live as Your woman.

Amen.

WANTED: A WIFE OF NOBLE CHARACTER

Debbie Kalmbach

A wife of noble character who can find?
She is worth far more than rubies.
Her husband has full confidence in her
and lacks nothing of value.
Proverbs 31:10–11

I caught my breath as I opened the tiny, velvet-covered box. Earrings sparkled; facets reflected the setting sunlight.

My husband beamed, obviously pleased he had surprised me for our anniversary. He had presented me with a waffle iron earlier that day. Although not too romantic, we needed a new one after twenty years. I appreciated his thoughtfulness. I hadn't expected another gift. Tears filled my eyes.

We had married at eighteen and become parents that first year. The adjustments and responsibilities had overwhelmed me. My husband, thoughtful and caring while we dated, now seemed to prefer time spent with friends, away from our cramped apartment, fussy baby, and his unhappy wife. Self-pity and resentment lurked as constant companions. As years passed, my look-at-all-I'm-doing attitude kept me miserable. Self-righteousness blinded me to my own shortcomings.

Then something happened that changed my life forever. I knelt on a cold, January day and asked Jesus to come into my life. "Please help me, Lord. I'm not doing so well at being a wife and mom. I can't do it myself," I prayed.

Change came slowly, painfully at times. Difficult circumstances chiseled the rough edges of my pride and self-sufficiency. I began reading God's Word and attending Bible study. I learned that God had a plan for me as wife and mother, not a dull, joyless task, but a special job He had entrusted to me. Unconditional love, acceptance, forgiveness, concepts I hadn't understood before, I now found new strength to accomplish.

The Lord helped me shift the focus from my husband's faults to looking honestly at mine. It meant being humble and letting go of pride and expectations. It meant simply committing myself to this man God had brought into my life.

Gradually the Lord breathed new life into our marriage. In time, I realized my husband had grown to be my dearest friend. Our marriage became a partnership. We began communicating to each other our feelings and needs; we enjoyed being together. Giving became a pleasure, not an obligation.

"Aren't you going to try the earrings on?" my husband asked, interrupting my thoughts. God in His goodness had given me everything I had hoped for in a husband, one who treasured me far more than precious gems.

Dear Lord, thank You for loving me enough to intervene in my life, for teaching me about being a godly wife, and for turning my pain and heartache into unmeasured joy.
Amen.

THE BIBLE STUDY

Nancy Kennedy

Pride goes before destruction,
a haughty spirit before a fall.
Proverbs 16:18

"Lord, what happened?" I cried. Surveying my living room, I saw that everything was picture-perfect for my Bible study. Earlier that morning I had vacuumed, polished the furniture, and carefully put away all my non-Christian books and magazines. Praise music filled the house. The aroma of French roasted coffee combined deliciously with the sweet smell of my freshly baked fish-shaped cookies that I had meticulously frosted with the ancient Christian symbol IXOYE.

What could possibly have gone wrong? Wasn't it my Christian duty to invite the "poor lost souls" in my neighborhood to a Bible study? After all, I knew so much about the Bible. (I'd been a Christian for three whole months!) Didn't they need me to teach them the truth?

"I don't understand, Lord!" I prayed. "I'm certain I did everything right!" I mentally went over my checklist again. I had bought them each a Bible (to show my Christian generos-

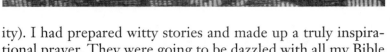

ity). I had prepared witty stories and made up a truly inspirational prayer. They were going to be dazzled with all my Bible knowledge, and awestruck at the way my face glowed as I talked about the Lord. (I had practiced in front of the mirror.)

I was going to tell the ladies, "Once I was lost, but now I'm found; was blind, but now I see." Then, I planned to tell them that they, too, could be like me. My plans were foolproof, except . . . nobody came!

After three hours passed, I poured out the coffee and laughed. "Fish-shaped cookies!" I roared.

God finally let me in on His little secret. In His merciful wisdom, He kept all those "poor lost souls" safe from my arrogance and pride. Proverbs 16:18 warns of the consequences of a haughty spirit. Sometimes I wonder if the Lord had me in mind when He wrote that. I certainly had a haughty spirit, and I certainly fell. But God mercifully picked me up again and let me have a wonderful laugh on myself.

My Bible study was over ten years ago. Am I still haughty and proud? How I would love to say that I'm not. I am, however, much more careful in checking my attitude whenever I'm involved in the Lord's work. If I ever see that I'm practicing my "spiritual glow" in front of the mirror, I immediately remember fish-shaped cookies and how nobody came to eat them.

Lord, if I'm filled with myself, I can't be filled
with You. Continue to show me my sinful
pride so that I might get out of the way
and let Your light shine through.
Amen.

"ARE YOU RUNNING WITH ME, GOD?"

Carla Anne Kirk

Let your eyes look directly ahead,
and let your gaze be fixed straight in front
of you. Watch the path of your feet, and all
your ways will be established.
Proverbs 4:25–26, NASB

Living the sanctified rat race—juggling my time between three boys, one man, and a two-story colonial—I often ask, "Are You running with me, God?"

Scripture tapes have become my means for hearing the Word, and prayer is tucked into the spare moments of my life: during traffic jams, in the shower, and over a sink full of dishes. My life has become a series of cantata and bell practice rehearsals, writing projects, housework, and running various errands for the boys.

Recently I took a scenic route home from carpooling the children to school. Too much to do in too little time had made me want to take a leisurely ride in the country.

When I reached the main highway, I noticed a Jeep on the northbound shoulder of the road. The owner was easy to spot as she ran along the roadway wearing a yellow slicker, white slacks, and a mandarin orange turtleneck sweater.

As I passed her, I watched curiously while she waved her arms and re-routed the northbound cars into the southbound lane. Since the cars that she was waving aside were veering into my path, I had to slip off the highway onto the roughly paved shoulder.

My car crept along as I watched the girl, who with confident authority could wield the drivers away from the object of her quest. *What would entice the girl to face such danger?*

Then I saw the turtle. Tears welled up in my eyes as I looked at the defenseless creature making its way across the road, oblivious to oncoming traffic. I felt as though that turtle represented me, inching along, my best efforts leading me into a lane of traffic and destruction.

Much like the turtle, I've made goals, set my course, and run the race, only to feel God plucking me up out of harm's way. At other times, God's will has sent me contrary to the heavy stream of traffic.

It would be easy to argue, then, that to err is human. But to see the divine is to see God redirecting traffic around my feeble frame.

Lord, thank You for plucking me up and

placing me back on the path of Your desire.

Amen.

HIS CONFIDENCE
CONQUERS FEAR

Berit Kjos

Do not be afraid . . .
for the LORD will be your confidence.
Proverbs 3:25–26, NASB

"Will you teach the Bible study next week?"

This simple request numbed my mind and turned my stomach. Nothing frightened me more than speaking in front of people. I didn't fear flying, earthquakes, or climbing mountains, but lead a group discussion? I couldn't do it. I didn't know enough. Leadership wasn't my gift.

"My Lord, You are not really asking this of me, are You?" On my knees, I pleaded for assurance that would restore my peace. But through the thunder of my throbbing heart, I heard Him whisper a Scripture He had just taught me, "Go, and I . . . will be with your mouth, and teach you what you are to say" (Ex. 4:12).

How could I say no?

Sleeplessness, anxiety, and dread stalked me until another Scripture came alive in my mind. I was reading 2 Corinthians

3:4–5, "Such confidence we have through Christ. . . . Not that we are adequate in ourselves . . . our adequacy is from God."

"Lord, give me this confidence," I prayed. "I can't do it, but You can." And He did. As I chose to rely on His strength rather than my feelings, His confidence began to loosen the paralyzing grip of fear and inadequacy. The next day, He led and spoke through my trembling body—the women heard Him, not me.

From then on, each faltering step, with Him leading, teaching, and speaking through me, proved that He could use a broken, willing vessel to demonstrate His faithfulness. I kept affirming Scriptures that emphasized God's participation in my life.

Jesus Christ is my wisdom; He knows what's best. He is my strength; nothing is impossible for Him. He is my holiness; and He will transform me according to His timing. Whenever feelings of fear revive and threaten to overwhelm me, which is often, He gently reminds me, "My grace is sufficient for you, for power is perfected in weakness" (2 Cor. 12:9).

Thank You, precious Lord, for giving me

confidence. You have shown me in Your

Word that no matter what You ask me

to be or to do, You will accomplish it.

How I praise You for that!

Amen.

FROM FEAR
TO FAITH

Beverly LaHaye

A rebuke goes deeper into one
who has understanding.

Proverbs 17:10, NASB

My husband and I started our life together involved in a local church. Because Tim was a pastor, I was immediately thrown into leadership. There I was, a young, fearful woman with a very poor self-image, pushed into playing the part of a skillful and capable pastor's wife.

The women looked to me to be a leader. I was expected to teach Bible classes, to play the organ, lead the choir, to stand up and pray eloquently in public, to bake the very best cakes—all this was, I thought, part of my new job description. Suddenly, I found myself thrust into an area in which I felt I was totally inadequate.

Instead of trying to sharpen up and meet these challenges and expectations, I retreated. Where I started out lacking confidence, I became downright fearful. And the more fearful I became, the more intimidated I felt.

During the early years of our ministry, I remember agreeing to give a devotional even though I was scared to death. A

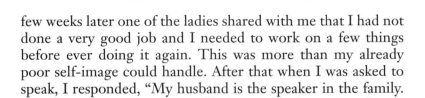

few weeks later one of the ladies shared with me that I had not done a very good job and I needed to work on a few things before ever doing it again. This was more than my already poor self-image could handle. After that when I was asked to speak, I responded, "My husband is the speaker in the family. I'm just his helpmeet."

One day I was abruptly brought face to face with what I was doing. We had been in the ministry fifteen or sixteen years. Throughout that time I had limited myself to teaching young children in Sunday School; only with them did I feel comfortable. Then one day Dr. Henry Brandt took me aside and pointed out 2 Timothy 1:7: "For God hath not given us the spirit of fear; but of power, and of love, and of a sound mind" (KJV). Then, without trying to spare my feelings, he told me, "Beverly, your fear is based on selfishness and that is a sin. You need to deal with it." A sin! I staggered.

Believe me, this was not easy to hear. When Dr. Brandt started repeating my own words back to me, just as I'd said them, I could see it all. It was obvious even to me.

In Romans 14:23, the apostle Paul tells us, "Whatever is not from faith is sin" (NASB). God wants us to walk by faith. But fear is not from faith; therefore, fear is sin.

Heavenly Father, it is not my desire to sin against You. I now know that fear is not of You; therefore, it is sin. From this day forward, I choose to walk by faith in the knowledge of Your Word and in the freedom You've given me through Your Son, Jesus Christ.

Amen.

CASTLES
VERSUS
MANSIONS

Erma Landis

Above all else, guard your heart,
for it is the wellspring of life.
Proverbs 4:23

We followed the tour guide through the castle-like mansion. A castle-like mansion? I asked our guide, "What's the difference between a castle and a mansion?"

"A mansion is meant for living," she replied. "It's a big house with many rooms. But a castle is meant primarily for defense."

Her answer clarified my thinking. She continued, "This house, though not built for defense, was built after the pattern of a castle. That is why turrets, like large bay windows, are on every floor. The turrets were originally made with vertical slits instead of windows. They widened on the inside wall so the soldiers would have a good vantage point to see the approaching enemy and could aim their fire accordingly. The turrets were built in circular columns that ran from the bottom floor to the top and were built on each side or corner of the structure."

As we were guided through the castle-designed mansion, I imagined the bay windows as the turrets the guide had men-

tioned, with cleverly placed slits instead of the elegant windows. What an excellent defense they would have been; a bullet would indeed have a hard time finding its way through those slits. In contrast to all the wars, struggles, and uncertainties the castles represented, a mansion is meant for living in peace, permanence, and plenty.

Then I realized, in a spiritual sense, we need our castles here below. We must have a strong defense against the attacks of Satan. We need the complete armor described in Ephesians 6. Neglecting to keep every piece of armor in good repair amounts to widening those vertical slits on the outside and narrowing them on the inside. In turn, this makes us more vulnerable to the devil's darts and less able to keep an effective lookout for his attacks.

Jesus is preparing mansions for us, not castles. Then our struggles will be over forever. The promised mansion will be an abiding place where we will live in His presence forever.

Lord, may I so guard my heart and
live my life that I will be a fit
occupant for the mansion
You are preparing for me.
Amen.

IN THE HOLLOW OF HIS HAND

Kathleen R. Lewis

Fear of man will prove to be a snare,
but whoever trusts in the LORD is kept safe.
Proverbs 29:25

The rain fell from a black sky in torrents of water so dense it was hard to see across the runway to the waiting plane. My family and I sat, delayed for several hours, at a small airport in East Java, Indonesia. The waiting was long but enjoyable, as we observed people and the ongoing entertainment my young granddaughter provided.

Our flight was moved forward again and again, even as the storm became more and more violent. Warily, I surveyed the weather, the clock, and the aircraft on the runway.

Daydreaming, my eyes again drifted around the walls of the terminal, this time seeing a large sign I hadn't noticed before. It was advertising a car rental service, but it was the bold headline that stopped me. "You couldn't be in safer hands," it read, in English! I knew immediately this sign was also a message for me, reminding me of my heavenly Father's loving care and

the utter safety of His will. Despite the drenching storm, our flight that day was smooth.

I have thought about that sign many times since then and the whole issue of the reliability of God's care versus our concepts of safety and danger. It's a wonderful thing to trust and rest in the One who holds all things together, who, despite our circumstances, is completely trustworthy. No matter where—whether in a familiar place or one fearfully strange—there is no safer place than in the center of God's will. That knowledge is more than enough for me.

A chorus from my childhood returns to me frequently. It tells of our God who keeps both day and night, who holds His children safe in the hollow of His hand.

There I rest, and there I stay.

Dear Father, thank You for the reliability of Your care, for the steadfastness of Your love for me, and for the safety of Your will that follows me wherever I may be. Help me to trust and follow with courage and hope.

Amen.

GREAT IS HIS FAITHFULNESS

Linda Miller

Honor the Lord from your wealth,
and from the first of all your produce;
so your barns will be filled with plenty,
and your vats will overflow with new wine.
Proverbs 3:9–10, NASB

I have found this principle to be true: Give to the Lord first and freely, and He gives back even more freely. I cannot out-give Him. It all belongs to Him anyway. Yet it is so easy to withhold a little for myself, especially when I want to make sure I have enough for an expense I know is coming.

I recall a few years ago when I was going to the Dominican Republic as a short-term summer missionary, and I needed to raise support money. One evening I was asked to speak at church along with three others who were going on various summer missions trips. We were to explain what we would be doing, where we were going, and what our goals and prayer needs were. Unknown to us, an offering was to be taken after our presentations to help meet some of our financial needs.

When the offering time came, and its focus was announced, I felt the Lord compelling me to be part of the offering. I tried to reason with the Lord and myself, saying it was ridiculous to give an offering, when the offering was being taken for me, and I had to be saving my money for my own trip. It didn't make sense! However, I had such a strong desire to give; I just knew it was from the Lord. I wrote a check for thirty dollars and placed it in the offering plate. When the service ended, a member of my Sunday School class approached me and handed me a check for my trip. It was for one hundred dollars! I just praise God for His faithfulness, and for reaffirming the principle that I can't outgive the Lord.

Lord, thank You for Your faithfulness in meeting my needs and for providing abundantly beyond them. Help me to be more faithful in giving to You first, withholding nothing.

Amen.

TASTE LIFE JUST FOR TODAY

Shirley Mitchell

Do not boast about tomorrow,
for you do not know what a day may bring forth.
Proverbs 27:1

One never deals directly with anything but the moment. The past is gone. The future is uncertain. But, each of us can concentrate upon the moment to fill it with greatness.

When my son was in third grade, he brought home a little saying he learned at school. It encouraged me to live moment by moment and went like this: Inch by inch, life's a cinch. Mile by mile, life is hard. God in His perfect wisdom only gives us one moment at a time.

I've made a list of seven ways I want to taste life, just for today:

Just for today, I will love the Lord, my God, with all my heart, with all my soul, with all my mind, and I will love my neighbor as myself.

Just for today, I will taste happiness. Abraham Lincoln once said that folks are just as happy as they make up their minds to be. Happiness does not depend on externals; it comes from within.

Just for today, I will keep my body totally fit. I will exercise, eat properly, and get enough rest. I will not let my heart be troubled. I will use methods to reduce stress.

Just for today, I will have a quiet time with my Creator. I will meditate on God's Word, pray, and listen. I will grow spiritually as I read material that will expand my mind and soul.

Just for today, I will have a positive attitude. I will not allow myself to be a victim of my circumstances. I will turn negative situations into positive ones.

Just for today, I'll move my life in the direction the Holy Spirit leads by making plans and following those plans.

Just for today, I will be good to myself, so I will feel like being good to others.

Lord, thank You for only giving me one moment at a time to deal with directly. With Your help, at the end of my life I will have a life full of great moments.

Amen.

GUIDANCE IN
THE GARDEN

Linda Montoya

Apply your heart to instruction,
and your ears to words of knowledge.

Proverbs 23:12, NAB

Margaret is my special friend. As a teenager, I had admired her from afar. She's a little bit older and wiser than I, a true pillar of society.

Recently, Margaret came over and knelt with me in my garden, not to pray, but to pull weeds. My beautiful garden that once produced lovely roses was now overgrown with neglect.

As Margaret and I knelt in the dirt that day, I had a profound sense of God's love and care for me. Margaret was talking about the rose garden while the Lord was instructing my heart.

"Always keep the center of the bush open," she said. "Remember to feed the plants and water them on a regular basis. It doesn't take much, just consistency."

I began to think of my spiritual life. Was the center of my focus on Jesus? Was I consistently taking time to be nourished and fed on the Word of God?

As my friend and I weeded our way through the garden, she continued, "A lot of these shoots have to be cut back and these suckers have to be removed."

In that instant, the Lord was showing me how my life, too, had become overgrown, in this case with a variety of activities. Wonderful and exciting as these activities might be, they were literally sucking the life out of me.

I realized that day that I needed to make some changes in how I care for my rose garden. I also needed to make some necessary changes in how I spend my time. My friend's kindness and guidance gave me renewed confidence that someday soon my garden, and my life, will bloom once again with vibrant living color.

Lord God, thank You for

speaking to me at times through

the words of a friend.

Amen.

THINGS AREN'T ALWAYS AS THEY APPEAR

Barbara L. Neiman

Let love and faithfulness never leave you;
bind them around your neck,
write them on the tablet of your heart.
Proverbs 3:3

It was after two in the morning, yet sleep eluded me. I decided to give up the fight and go out into the living room and read for awhile.

When I entered, moonlight flooded the room through the cathedral windows. I watched feathery snowflakes float past the windows for a moment before the thought entered my mind, *Snowflakes in May?*

I reached for the deck light. It took a moment for the sight of wispy, white, cottonwood fluff from the neighbor's trees floating like feathers to register in my mind. *Things aren't always as they appear,* the quiet, inner voice prompted.

As I padded back to bed in my bare feet, I thought, *Lord, what do those words mean? It must really be important for You to show me in this manner.*

I was ill and had been bedridden for the past ten months, so I had an abundance of time to reflect on my life. I began to sus-

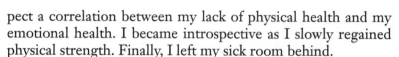

pect a correlation between my lack of physical health and my emotional health. I became introspective as I slowly regained physical strength. Finally, I left my sick room behind.

Deeply grateful to have my freedom again, I enrolled in a creative writing course. As I wrote I made a surprising discovery. I found the power of the pen to heal many of the wounds of my childhood.

For my first assignment, I wrote a story in which a baby girl was given a welcoming party by her older sister and brother. Somehow, I had never felt received by my siblings.

When the story was finished, I realized that as a child I'd had no idea of age-appropriate behavior, so I had often judged others unfairly. I had expected children, age four and under, to give me some kind of royal welcome. However, writing the story helped me acknowledge my feelings and see the lack of love and faithfulness that I'd extended because of my own immaturity.

Proverbs 3:3 made me aware that as a child I'd written many hurtful things on the tablet of my heart. Now was the time to deal with them.

Jesus, erase all distorted messages from my past. Help me write true love letters on the tablet of my heart so my actions will reflect Your faithfulness.

Amen.

HOPE
DEFERRED

Nancy Willis O'Meara

Hope deferred makes the heart sick,
but a longing fulfilled is a tree of life.
Proverbs 13:12

"I feel so lonely . . . even angry. He's hardly home and when he is, he's either asleep or reading a stupid medical journal," she said as she blew her nose. "I'm just tired of hoping and being disappointed."

"I feel angry and disappointed, too." I sighed as I handed Mary her coffee and more tissue. Her comments made me think about the night before.

I had prepared a romantic dinner for my husband who had been on call at the hospital the previous seventy-two hours. After sitting down, I lit the candles, and then we heard that wretched sound, "BEEP BEEP BEEP." It was my husband's beeper going off again, which meant go directly to the hospital, do not collect dinner. I wept as I watched his headlights back out of the driveway. Hope deferred makes the heart sick, and this internship was beginning to make me feel terminally ill.

I found it surprising that I felt angry, disappointed, and so alone during my husband's medical training. I had heard those medical horror stories about interns working 125 hours a week, and I had vowed to be supportive of my husband when and if those demands were placed on him.

But in reality, I was angry. My expectations of marriage weren't being met. I found myself crying out to God. The more alone I felt, the more I leaned on God, yearning for strength and peace. God supported me as I became overwhelmed with life and began to devour Scripture, in search of hope.

I was not disappointed. The Bible came alive with the footprints of men and women who had struggled with the same realities of life that I was now facing. Slowly, I began to soften and look more to my heavenly Father rather than my exhausted husband to meet my needs. My circumstances were not changing, but I was.

Thank You, Lord, for using life's

frustrating disappointments to draw me back

to You. Help me to realize that only You can

meet my inner longings and give me hope.

Amen.

A
PROVERB FOR
SUPERMOMS

Glenda Palmer

Her children rise up and call her blessed.

Proverbs 31:28, RSV

If Proverbs 31 were written for the modern woman, I think it might read something like this, beginning with verse 10:

(10) If you can find a truly good wife, she is worth more than all the diamonds in Tiffany's!

(11) She listens to Christian radio instead of watching the afternoon soaps.

(12) She holds the flashlight and doesn't make fun when her husband repairs the drippy plumbing for the seventh time.

(13) She sews on Girl Scout patches while watching Sesame Street with her four-year-old,

(14) And treats her teenaged son's basketball team to pizza after they lose the big game.

(15) She gets up before dawn to go jogging, after setting out the box of oat bran and fresh fruit for her family.

(16) She earns a real estate license and puts a down payment on a duplex with her commission check.

(17) She keeps her floors shiny with Mop 'n' Sop,

(18) And shops at garage sales.

(19) She writes the monthly bills while watching the eleven o'clock news,

(20) And cleans out her closets for the homeless.

(21) She enjoys knitting sweaters while watching Monday night football with her #1 hero.

(22) When she gets dressed up, her king of the castle thinks she looks like a queen.

(23) Once she and her husband attended the White House Prayer Breakfast,

(24) And she didn't faint when the president of the United States shook her hand.

(25) She works out at "believer-cize" and softens her skin with vitamin E oil.

(26) She smiles and says "Good morning" to the cranky next-door neighbor.

(27) She keeps score for her son's Little League games and agrees to teach Sunday School one more year. She goes to PTA meetings and choir practice, even when it means missing the conclusion to a mini-series she is following.

(28) Her husband tells her, "Honey, you're the greatest," and her children rise up and call her . . . collect.

Lord, help me become a good example for my
children to follow and a reward for my
husband to cherish.
Amen.

HOLY LAUGHTER AND HOLY DUSTPANS

Aurora Presley

Anxiety in the heart of a man weighs it down,
but a good word makes it glad.
Proverbs 12:25, NASB

I had just completed chairing an event for the women in our church in which I had played a major leadership role. The event had God's blessing on it, and lives had been changed beyond any of our prayers and planning.

Yet now I found a sea of complete exhaustion drowning out the blessing and, in the process, washing away my perspective. Though I could see what was transpiring, I needed additional prayer support to give me added strength as we were all coming down from this massive project.

I found myself traveling to the home of a friend. I knew I needed prayer, and soon, before I dissolved into a puddle of tears.

After a warm greeting and a few comments, we began to pray. Within moments I heard my friend praying, "And, Lord, we know that in Your eyes Aurora is just a speck of dust . . ." Suddenly, I found myself dissolving into laughter. I couldn't stop myself. All I could see was a picture of a tiny speck of dust trying to hold up the world and stumbling under the ridiculous load. Somehow in the light of that perspective, I saw my foolishness, and nothing else at that moment mattered. It really was all in Father God's hands, not in mine.

I was released instantly from the distortion I had been battling, and a new perspective settled deep in my heart. I couldn't stop laughing, and now my friend had caught my laughter, too. It was a holy laughter that cleansed the wrong thinking of my mind and wrapped the deeper recesses of my soul with the joy of God's perspective.

Somehow I did not feel insignificant through this insight, just completely cared for and loved. Perhaps it was because the perspective had hit me that my world and all it holds is really in my Lord's hands. A speck of dust cannot hold up the world.

Thank goodness, my loving, heavenly Father can . . . and He does!

Father God, how delightful that You so
quickly can turn my perspective around.
Help me reach through to the gift of Your
Spirit for the view You want me to have of
my life. And thank You for laughter.
In Your wonderful name.
Amen.

AWESOME SEA, AWESOME GOD

Mary Proctor

When he gave the sea its boundary so the
waters would not overstep his command,
and when he marked out the
foundations of the earth.
Proverbs 8:29

A light mist shrouded me as I jogged slowly on the empty beach. It was a gray, overcast day. Now and then I paused, enthralled by the power of the rushing sea. Waves rolled in, then out, swirling away bits of shells, rocks, and debris almost faster than my eyes could track them. I stared intently at them, then moved on, my bare feet thudding against the soaked sand.

After a while, my legs, unused to the terrain, screamed for relief. I walked in the surf then and surveyed the shoreline.

Ultra-modern hotels, like gawky science-fiction androids, dwarfed weathered, rustic beach houses. Standing side by side, they starkly contrasted each other against the threatening sky. Like silent sentries, many were perched on stilt-like structures to fend off the unrelenting assaults of the sea.

A wave crashed violently against my legs, momentarily thrusting me off balance. I regained my composure, then

braced myself to reexamine the frothy surf. Could there be any treasures hidden in it for me? If so, I had only seconds to spot and scoop up whatever caught my eye. I strained to locate the surging objects.

Suddenly something glistened in the foam. Darting down, I snatched a colorful prize, then another, and another, and stuffed them in my pockets. Bit by bit, I gathered tiny rocks, shells, and driftwood and balanced them against my chest. Soon I could not stash another item. I turned toward home.

Walking slowly now, my senses felt charged with the wonder and awesomeness of the sea. Yet more than that, its endless rhythm, riches, and power reminded me of the eternal faithfulness and majesty of God. Tears welled in my eyes as I considered His goodness and love for me. Praise burst from my heart in grateful response. Oh, that all men might love and worship Him!

> *Lord, may I never cease to remember who You*
> *are, and thank You for Your mighty works*
> *and enduring love.*
> *Amen.*

PRIDE PRECEDES A FALL

Ruth M. Rink

Pride goes before destruction,
and a haughty spirit before stumbling.
Proverbs 16:18, NASB

Feeling rather pleased with my testimony given as a guest in another church, I turned to leave the pulpit where a small stool had been placed to accommodate my four-foot, eleven-inch height. Plop! Down I went. A gasp from the congregation exploded in my ears as I landed on my backside, note cards still clutched in my moist hands.

"How foolish!" I muttered to myself. "Is my skirt in place? What are people thinking?"

In a flash, the pastor was at my side, helping me up and easing me to the front pew. I stared straight ahead, too embarrassed to do anything else. As the service continued, I slowly began to relax and then to giggle inwardly as I realized that once again pride had jeopardized my eighty-year-old dignity.

I've struggled with an exaggerated sense of self-importance often during these eight decades; this was one more instance

when pride threatened to undo me, despite many lessons to the contrary in the past.

But just as the local junior high school continues to produce literate students without my presence in Room 314, and just as the church choir still touches hearts without the aid of my alto voice, and just as the Women's Mission Society has proven quite capable of presenting splendid programs and fund-raisers without my valuable insights, I've learned that no one is indispensable, not even me!

What do I have of which to be proud? Nothing, really. All I have and all I am are gifts of grace from the Lord Jesus. He doesn't judge me on the basis of my accomplishments in the classroom or my activities as a church member. He accepts me just as I am—falls and all!

Father, forgive me for my foolish pride
and keep me constantly aware of
my need of You.
Amen.

GOOD MEDICINE

Ruth Robinson-LaFreniere

A cheerful heart is good medicine.
Proverbs 17:22

I'll never forget that Sunday morning in 1983. It was my first time to go to church since my two-month stay in the hospital following a five-hour brain surgery that left me a hemiplegic, with a one-sided paralysis.

I had just taken a new pair of control-top panty hose out of the package, using my teeth and right hand, and was staring at the incredibly tiny legs that somehow were to fit my now overweight body.

With the help of my eleven- and twelve-year-old daughters and my husband, I huffed and puffed, grunted and pulled, until finally the panty hose were on. With a sigh of relief and feeling of accomplishment, I sat down. At that very moment, my youngest daughter's ring caught on the front of my nylons, sending a huge run up the front of my leg.

Our eyes locked in a stare of disbelief and horror at what had just happened! Then all at once we exploded into laughter.

I have found that laughter—even laughing at myself—is such a release from the heavy, serious stuff of life that we all experience.

Our Lord knew that life would not always be easy and lighthearted. In fact, the apostle Paul said, "For it has been granted to you on behalf of Christ not only to believe on him, but also to suffer for him" (Phil. 1:29).

I am learning that laughter—as well as tears—is good medicine in the healing process going on inside of me. And I'm grateful for these instructions from God's Word that bring health to my body, soul, and spirit.

Dear heavenly Father, help me to find joy and humor in the tough stuff of life. Thank You that You use laughter to help heal the pain and hurts that are a part of my journey.

Amen.

FLOUNDERING FISH

Dorethea Schauber

Do not withhold good from those who deserve it,
when it is in your power to act.
Proverbs 3:27

Early one morning as I walked along the seashore and as the surf lapped at my feet, I saw many small fish washed ashore by the rolling waves and left floundering. The sea gulls swayed and glided silently above the shore; they swooped down, picked up the small fish only to consume them.

As I continued to walk, I noticed one small fish washed up on the sand. After many assists by the waves of the sea, it was left stranded on the sand. I approached the exhausted fish and used the toes of my right foot to scoop down under it and lift it into the wave, which finally put it back into its "swim of life."

This little scenario reminded me of how we as children of God sometimes get stranded on the sands of time and find ourselves floundering in the sea of life. As the sea gulls consume the stranded fish, so Satan, the enemy of our soul,

swoops in to destroy those whom the tides of circumstance wear down.

Our kind, loving heavenly Father wants us to be sensitive to those around us, those who have been washed ashore by the waves of life that can crush, damage, and destroy. He wants us to reach down into the mire and lift out that one who is stranded, washed up, or wiped out. Jesus wants us to be that wave of love, His love flowing through us to those who are bruised and hurting and in need of a soothing wave to bring them back into the stream of His will.

Father, help me be that vessel through whom

Your wave of love may flow, reaching to those

who need to once again experience

Your love and healing.

Amen.

GOD CARES ABOUT TURKEYS!

Marilyn Zent Schlitz

Better a meal of vegetables where there is love
than a fattened calf with hatred.
Proverbs 15:17

Fall was the slow season in our little tourist town, when hours were cut and income levels plummeted. Each Thanksgiving I juggled finances, trying to figure out how to provide the traditional turkey dinner with all the trimmings.

One year relatives were coming to share the holiday with my four children and myself. I had seventeen extra dollars—and no turkey! That Saturday night before Thanksgiving, I cried out to God, asking Him to help me feed seven people a holiday meal with seventeen dollars. Did God care whether we had turkey? Should I care so much?

That night's Scripture reading included the verse from Proverbs, "Better a meal of vegetables where there is love." Ouch! The rod of God's discipline stung my heart. Maybe an unusual holiday meal would be fun. Corn on the cob, fresh beans, baked potatoes with toppings. Seventeen dollars

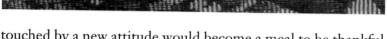

touched by a new attitude would become a meal to be thankful for.

Sunday afternoon there was a knock at the door. A stranger peeked around a huge box. "Are you Schlitz? I'm from the food bank. Someone gave us your name." I gasped as he eased the brimming box to the floor. Treasure! Riches! A turkey, a ham, potatoes, yams, cranberry sauce, pie shells, canned pumpkin. My spirit soared as I realized that God did care about our traditions and the desires of our hearts.

That night after church a deacon came running toward me, struggling with a big brown bag. "Marilyn, wait! Don't forget your turkey!" A second turkey. Blessings beyond measure. God was proving to me and to my observant children that He supplies our every need—and more!

Tuesday after work, a fellow employee came to me and put a turkey in my arms. "I just want to do this for you; don't say anything." She walked away before seeing the flood of tears— tears of gratitude for a generous friend, but more than that, tears of awe toward a personal, loving God who was showering me with affirmations of His presence. "Lord, thank You. And, Lord, You can stop sending turkeys!"

Lord, if I can pray, why should I worry? Bring
Your promises of provision to my mind daily.
Don't let me forget the turkeys!
Amen.

CALICO
ANGEL WINGS

Marcia Schwartz

*Through love and faithfulness sin is atoned for;
through the fear of the LORD a man avoids evil.*
Proverbs 16:6

Blond hair cascaded from the top knot of First Angel, who was rehearsing busily for the Christmas pageant. In her white gown made from an old sheet by her mother, she was hopping about, arms spread-eagled, trying out her new cardboard wings.

The celestial bliss was soon interrupted though, as cardboard wings dangled from their perilous string attachment. Running to her mother, she mourned, "Mommy, my wings keep falling off!"

Oh, Lord, my heart echoed, *so do mine.* My saintly Christian angel wings keep falling off. So often I fail Him. So often I shed my wings in disobedience and selfishness. Just the other day I lost my cool with some disruptive teenaged boys in my classroom and hurled words at them that weren't gracious Christian terms. Sometimes I gossip and say things I

shouldn't. My mouth gets me into a lot of trouble, and I constantly feel my wings slipping off.

Sometimes I am slow to have compassion for the poor, the disadvantaged of the world. I'm too wrapped up in my own desires and obsessions, and I know it's stupid and evil not to love God with my whole mind and heart and soul!

Sometimes my wings really are stiff cardboard wings that will not fly to do the Lord's will. Too often, they are only ordinary calico wings, not the splendid, gossamer type that propel God's mighty angels.

Mine are only human, earthbound calico wings, struggling in their faith, nothing rare and heavenly. I need the Lord to keep me trudging on, never giving up, seeking always Him and His will. When my wings become faded or wrinkled, God can restore them. He can empower these poor, awkward flapping things by the wings of the Holy Spirit. The Lord's love encourages my common, ordinary faith and helps it to grow. He also cares for that little blond angel hopping about and can encourage her faith, too.

> *Dear Father, who created little girl angels,*
> *me, the universe, faith, and love, keep me*
> *close to You this day. Deliver me from*
> *evil and help my faith to grow.*
> *Amen.*

A BROKEN CANDLE

Sandy Sheppard

A man's spirit will endure sickness;
but a broken spirit who can bear?
Proverbs 18:14, RSV

As a college student I attended an evening service beside a reservoir near campus. Darkness fell, and each of us was given a candle. I examined mine closely and found that it was broken all the way through. I could move the two halves slightly, but the wick held them together.

I thought about handing it in and asking for another candle, but then the flame was passed to me. I watched as the wick caught fire.

My candle burned just as brightly as the others. Its glow was unaffected by the break in the wax. A candle's purpose is to give light in the darkness, I thought, and mine fulfills its purpose just as well as a whole one.

Soon melted wax began dripping down the sides of the candle, until the break line was covered. The candle appeared whole, and the coating of wax held the sections steady.

We're all like that candle in some way. Broken by life, our spirits have been shattered time and again by circumstances we cannot change or control: divorce, abuse, fractured relationships, failure, illness, even gossip.

But God does not expect us to bear our broken spirits alone. He has provided Christ to be the wick that holds our wounded lives together. If we allow His flame to be ignited in our hearts, we will be changed forever. His love will flow down over our wounds, covering and healing them, restoring our wholeness with His touch. We will become stronger for what we have experienced. The glowing flame of Christ's love in us can dispel the darkness as we light the way for others to find the healing they need.

Broken candles can still burn brightly. Broken people can be a light to the world.

Dear Father, I come to You for Your love,
which covers and heals my brokenness. Make
me a light to those around me, leading others
to You for Your healing touch.
Amen.

READING HIS MANUAL

Janet Colsher Teitsort

Obey me and live! Guard my words as your
most precious possession. Write them down,
and also keep them deep within your heart.
Proverbs 7:2–3, TLB

Some of my Bible study friends and I were sitting around discussing how God guides us. One of the ladies spoke up and said, "The Bible is my manual. That's how God guides me. You know, we always read the manuals that come with our appliances."

Quickly a din arose as the other ladies raised skeptical eyebrows, exclaiming simultaneously, "We do?"

I went on to comment that I never read my manuals unless something breaks down. The truth is I never became an avid Bible reader until the Lord allowed me to become broken in spirit.

I remember praying to the Lord and asking forgiveness for my disobedience. I knew I had come to the end of myself. I needed to surrender every area of my life, not just the ones that I chose to give Him. There was to be no compromise.

As I renewed my commitment, the Lord impressed upon my mind the firm command to open His Word and learn of Him. It was then that I got out my manual, dusted it off, and began studying the "how-to" principles of God.

Looking back, I can see that my sporadic reading of God's Word hampered my spiritual growth. During the years that I had read the Bible so sparingly, Satan was able to keep me a defeated Christian. Now I am immersed in God's teachings. In fact, He has changed me so much that I barely recognize the person I used to be. He has put His commandments deep within my heart.

I have found that living a life by God's principles has many advantages. When I seek to do His will, He floods my life with His peace. I have His promise that He is guiding my steps, that His wisdom is always before me.

What pain and heartache I could have spared myself, my family, and most of all, the Holy Spirit. How I wish I had been more like the lady in my group who always reads the manual first.

Father, I want to be in Your manual daily, lest

I end up in brokenness and defeat.

Amen.

REALITY,
NOT ILLUSION

Faye Hill Thompson

Put all your trust in the LORD and do not rely on your own understanding. Think of him in all your ways, and he will smooth your path.
Proverbs 3:5–6, NEB

Now in my early forties, a victim of post polio, I sat in the doctor's office with my husband. For the first time during the course of our married life we were hearing the words, "You can have a baby if you want to." We were overwhelmed!

The following day my doctor phoned. "I've been thinking through our conversation yesterday. We didn't discuss fully the risks involved. The chances for you having an abnormal child are much greater at your age. This coupled with your previous condition would make you a high-risk pregnancy. It isn't that it can't be done. The other times you were told you couldn't; this time *you* control the decision."

During the succeeding days I probed the questions raised by this conversation.

"You will know," my pastor kept reassuring me. "Your answer will come in a seemingly unimportant moment."

As difficult as it was, I tried to keep my mind focused on Christ, asking what He would have me to do. Still no answer came.

Talking with my husband late one night, I erupted with frustration, "If only I were ten years younger and knew what I do now."

"Why are you trusting yourself with the decision anyway?" questioned my husband. "Why don't you turn it over to God completely? Maybe it would help if you went with me to my convention. The ladies' brunch is going to include a style show put on by a theater company featuring costumes from past productions."

Taking my husband up on his suggestion, I went with him to the convention. Near the end of the show, a middle-aged actress came out in a faded, adolescent party dress. The narrator explained, "And here's a character living in illusion, caught up in a vision of loveliness whose time is passed."

Suddenly I saw myself mirrored in this person. I knew the answer. I was liberated from my vision of loveliness, a pregnancy whose time had passed. In a seemingly unimportant moment, God had smoothed my path.

Help me, Lord, not to lament

what could have been but

rather rejoice in what is.

Amen.

WORN SPOTS

Doris Toppen

*"Behold, I will pour out my Spirit on you;
I will make my words known to you."*
Proverbs 1:23, NASB

The rich fragrance of used apple crates rotting in the August heat invaded my senses and transported me back to the wide sunshine of childhood. In my mind, I could see the rope swing that Dad had made for me and feel the warm, dry grass and gnarled roots under my feet as I snuggled my plump bottom onto the notched wooden seat. Over and over again Dad would give me a push, encourage me, and straighten the rope when I steered crooked.

The rugged rope buffed the insides of my hands as I pushed off across the spot where my tracks had rubbed the grass away. Swinging high into the top of the maple, I could almost see to heaven, made friends with the clouds, and told my secrets to God. It was a holy place where I wore that spot down and pumped even higher until I could see my dreams coming true. I swallowed the wind and the wonder, and I soared until the last call for supper.

The shine of the worn spots of my youth remains fresh: the pathway to school, to the pasture, to the creek, and to Judy's house. I choose to push off from savored memories in joy—a joy that God gives to soften some of the blows that are thrust, when darkness shuts my world down and I feel like a baseball in the ditch with the seams torn open.

Sometimes I need a loving push from God, a tightening of the ropes. Lured by God to the top of the hills and mountains in my life, I try to see beyond the struggle and pump fiercely, to hold on though scratched and blistered until I feel new confidence in my dreams.

I am encouraged to remember where I've been, to touch and learn from the spent places that tell my story, and to look to the challenges just around the next corner.

So I push off across the finished spots of youth, tree houses, motherhood, and middle-age, through the years of traffic tramping across my soul, and find moments that stand still. And I taste the fragrance of childhood, the freshness of today, and the sharp joy of being alive.

Lord, let me pump with childlike enthusiasm
as You help me to see wisdom and power
in the worn away spots in my life, to
embrace the challenges and to
push forward to new places.
Amen.

RAGGED
EDGES

Marcy Weydemuller

*"Blessed is the man who listens to me, watching
daily at my gates, waiting at my doorposts."*
Proverbs 8:34, NASB

A sense of peacefulness flows softly through me as I stand
on the craggy bluff overlooking battered cliffs. Today they
sparkle in the gentle, warm sunlight.

Low-flying seagulls hover, then sway lightly with the calm,
rolling waves. Some gulls circle quickly upward, then swoop
downward toward the floating kelp patches.

Miniature fishing boats dot the horizon. Behind them a
thick, wide fog bank lingers on the edge, waiting to return to
the shore and carpet this bluff in its mists.

A gentle breeze tickles my face and turns the meadow
behind me into grass dancers rippling and bowing to hidden
wildflowers. I'm in a live postcard today, lazy and timeless.

*Why, Lord? Why can't each day be peaceful and calm, alone with
You?* Lately I'm seeking a sense of tranquillity, but instead I
erupt with raw nerves.

These last few months have been filled with tense emotions and constant noise pounding my mind and senses. I don't even have a small crisis to blame; it's just daily living battering me down.

The craggy bluff shows tourists like me its softer nature, but I remember other days when I have heard the waves pounding against the rocks below. These battered sides didn't form from gentle days. Their beauty came from wind and waves cutting harsh scars into their sides, not just once in a while but day after day.

I've been ignoring that, haven't I, Lord? Instead of looking for rest from conflict, I should be seeking God's purpose and His strength to guide me when I am buffeted.

When I do seek the Lord, I find an inner calmness that sustains me throughout His shaping and molding. And I, too, can only grow piece by piece and day by day.

> *Thank You, Lord, for reminding me to*
> *continually seek Your face and Your*
> *strength to meet the daily*
> *challenges.*
> *Amen.*

REGULAR
CHECK-UPS
RECOMMENDED

Jan Watrous Woodard

*The integrity of the upright guides them, but
the unfaithful are destroyed by their duplicity.*
Proverbs 11:3

Blond hair flowing, a slender young woman breezed out of
the doctor's office as I entered for my regular check-up. Her
pleasing looks lingered in the back of my mind as I sat in the
crowded waiting room, browsing through a dog-eared
women's magazine.

When my examination finally began, I referred to his previous patient and asked my doctor, a strong, Christian family
man, "How do you handle being around so many attractive
women?"

"It's simple," he replied. He pointed to the examining table,
and I hopped up. Thumping my knee with a little hammer, he
said, "Whenever I feel the slightest attraction toward another
woman, I tell my wife about my thoughts that day. Immediate
honesty with her prevents me from ever moving beyond that
first thought."

I pondered our conversation as I peeled potatoes for dinner after returning home. My doctor's comments reminded me that Jesus said sin originates in the heart.

What may be growing in my own heart? I challenged myself. How often do I fail to recognize and flee temptations when they first appear? For instance, could those occasional yearnings for affluence and success, freeing me from the monotony of dishes, laundry, and car pools, threaten to put down tiny roots of discontent in my life?

Those are just momentary, little daydreams, I protested inwardly. *Ah, but with the potency to seduce you away from faithfulness to God!* my conscience whispered back.

Standing at my kitchen sink, I admitted to myself the need for regular spiritual check-ups to counter the pull of temptations. Just as my doctor safeguards his healthy marriage and his personal integrity by remaining totally honest before his wife, I want to remain spiritually candid before my God.

Because my intimacy with the Lord is too important to risk forfeiting for some fleeting pleasure, I now regularly spend time alone with Him, asking Him to search my heart. I've learned as I faithfully confess my weaknesses, temptations lose their power to entice me away from His best for my life.

Great Physician, search and cleanse my heart

again today. Keep me alert to temptations

that would lure me away from Your love.

Amen.

ECHO WORDS

Bobbie Yagel

Death and life are in the power of the tongue.
Proverbs 18:21, RSV

Dull, dark hair framed the young woman's angular face. Occasionally she peeked at me from beneath heavy bangs covering her eyebrows. As tears trickled down her cheeks, she sputtered the words spoken to her twenty-five years previously by her elementary school principal.

"'Why can't you be more like your smart brother?' he demanded as I stood in front of his desk, knees knocking, wondering why I'd been called to his office. 'He's an excellent student. But just look at your miserable grades!'"

Dabbing at her eyes with a tissue, she took a deep breath, sighed, and summed up her years of compounded failures. "I still ask myself that question every day."

The principal's words, which echo down the dark hallway of my friend's life, remind me of words first spoken to me at age eight as I stood in front of our small, brick Baptist church in Richmond, Virginia. My toothpick legs wobbled from

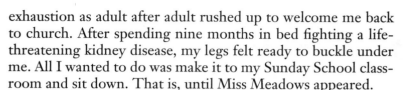

exhaustion as adult after adult rushed up to welcome me back to church. After spending nine months in bed fighting a life-threatening kidney disease, my legs felt ready to buckle under me. All I wanted to do was make it to my Sunday School classroom and sit down. That is, until Miss Meadows appeared.

This retired missionary lady was a bit of a toothpick herself. Impeccably dressed in a navy suit, her white hair tucked tightly in a bun at the nape of her neck, she smiled, stooped down until we were eye to eye, and placed her frail hand under my chin.

"Bobbie Lee Brown," she drawled in her Virginia accent, "God saved you for a special purpose." And then, having etched on my mind with indelible ink her encouraging words, she disappeared into the church.

In "Family Happiness Is Homemade," Eric Hoffman writes, "It is not so much the example of others we imitate, as the reflection of ourselves in their eyes and the echo of ourselves in their words" (*Family Concern*, Wheaton, Ill., Jan. 1986).

I can only imagine the scowling face and sharp voice of the elementary principal whose words still echo in the ears of the young woman with heavy bangs and a heavy burden of life.

How blessed I feel to see myself in the echo of Miss Meadow's words and the lilt of her voice. Spoken fifty-five years ago, her ten words inspire me daily to humbly ask, "Lord, what is Your purpose for my life this day?"

Dear Father, help me encourage with words of
life each person You bring my way today.
Amen.

MEET OUR CONTRIBUTORS

Barbara Anderson is a homemaker. Several of her poems have been published. She enjoys writing, sewing, painting, and playing the piano. She and her husband, Harlan, have three grown children and two grandchildren and live in Danville, Calif.

Niki Anderson is a church secretary and the author of several magazine articles, devotions, interviews, and Sunday School take-home papers. She enjoys biking and home decorating. Niki and her husband, Bob, have two children and make their home in Spokane, Wash.

Betty L. Arthurs is a homemaker and freelance writer. A member of the Tempe Christian Writers' Group, she has written children's short stories and magazine fillers and articles. Betty enjoys reading, swimming, music, and playing with her grandson. She and her husband, John, have two grown children and live in Tempe, Ariz.

Leslie B. Bagg is a published poet who enjoys gardening, tole painting, cross-stitch, reading, and Bible study and teaching. She is a homemaker and part-time substitute teacher. Leslie and her husband, Barney, have two grown sons and one grandchild. The Baggs make their home in Beaumont, Calif.

Victoria J. Bastedo is a homemaker who enjoys writing devotions and poetry, reading, and kayaking. She and her husband, Rick, have three young children and make their home in Snoqualmie, Wash.

Faye L. Braley has written poetry and is the editor and contributing author of *The Secretary's Manual* (Assoc. of Christian Schools Int.). Her hobbies include quilting, knitting, yard work, gardening, reading, and cooking. She and her husband, Jim, have two adult children and reside in Cottonwood, Ariz.

Irene B. Brand is a retired school teacher who has written eleven novels, including *Heartstrings* (Barbour) and several as *Guideposts'* Forever Romance bookclub selections, and four non-fiction titles. She enjoys walking, traveling, crocheting, and being active in her church. Irene and her husband, Rob, reside in Southside, W. Va.

Shirley Brosius has written several devotions and articles and is a freelance newspaper writer. Her hobbies include reading and walking. She and her husband have two grown sons and one daughter, Christy, who went to be with the Lord in 1975. The Brosius' reside in Millersburg, Pa.

Karen Carncross is a devotional writer and counselor. Her hobbies include playing the piano, writing music, reading, and hiking. She has one son and resides in Bainbridge Island, Wash.

Annie Chapman is a Christian songwriter, author, and homemaker. Author of *Smart Women Keep it Simple* (Bethany House, 1992), she and her husband, Steve, have recorded ten albums. They perform musically nationwide promoting a message on the family.

Jeri Chrysong is a legal word processor who has written a variety of devotions, articles, and poems. Her hobbies are baseball with the kids, writing, weekend travel, dream chasing, church choir, and country music concerts. She has two sons and resides in Huntington Beach, Calif.

Linda Clare has had her articles and poetry published in several magazines and newspapers. Formerly a teacher, she is now a freelance writer who enjoys reading, textile art, and doing art projects with her children. Linda and her husband have four children and live in Eugene, Ore.

Patti Townley Covert has written several magazine articles and devotions. She is self-employed as a typist, as well as a freelance writer. She enjoys gardening, Jazzercise, being on the beach, reading, and serving as secretary for Bible Study Fellowship. Patti and her husband, Jim, have two sons and reside in Ontario, Calif.

Betty Edwards is a retired missionary who enjoys quilting, sewing, crafts, and teaching women's Bible studies. She is a conference speaker and former area director of Aglow Women's Ministries, as well as YWAM director. Betty and her husband, Jack, have five children and twelve grandchildren and live in Santa Rosa, Calif.

Elisabeth Elliot has written over twenty-eight books and hosts the radio program *Gateway to Joy*. Elisabeth is a former missionary to the Auca Indians. She has two grown daughters, and she and her husband, Lars, have eight grandchildren.

Remi Adeeko Enobakhare is a full-time homemaker, part-time substitute teacher, and home-schooler. Remi enjoys reading, writing, and studying foreign languages and cultures. She and her husband, Ede, have two young children and reside in Camarillo, Calif.

Marjorie K. Evans is a retired school teacher, now a homemaker and freelance writer, who has numerous articles and devotions published. Marjorie enjoys grandparenting, reading, traveling, needlework, and tending to nearly two hundred potted plants. The Evans have two grown sons and five grandchildren and live in Irvine, Calif.

Kira Love Flores is a full-time homemaker who enjoys writing, reading, journaling, and the great outdoors of the Pacific Northwest. She and her husband have two daughters and make their home in Kingston, Wash.

Martha E. Garrett, former Christian bookstore manager and Christian college executive secretary, enjoys writing, walking, photography, and writing letters and postcards. She has four adult children, ten grandchildren, five great-grandchildren and resides in East Wenatchee, Wash.

Wilma Brown Giesser has written many devotions and articles. She is a retired technical writer and now is a freelance writer and volunteer for her church. She enjoys travel trailering, reading, spending time with her grandchildren, and writing as a legacy for her family. She and her husband, Donald, have three children and seven grandchildren and live in Sacramento, Calif.

Sonya D. Gore is a homemaker and freelance writer who enjoys writing, sewing, and reading. Sonya and her husband, Larry, have two children and make their home in Ninnekah, Okla.

Ruth Bell Graham is the author of several books, including *Sitting by My Laughing Fire* and *Prodigals and Those Who Love Them*. Wife of evangelist Billy Graham, she and her family live in Montreat, N.C. The Grahams have five children.

Carlene Hacker has written numerous articles, devotions, and poems, and has received several writing awards. She is also a speaker and classroom music teacher. Carlene and her husband have three children and make their home in San Diego, Calif.

Lynn Hallimore is a homemaker and freelance writer with over thirty-five articles to her writing credit. She enjoys watercolor painting, home decorating, camping, bike riding, walking, and drama. Lynn and her husband, John, have two children and live in Cameron Park, Calif.

Freya Ottem Hanson is a lawyer and the author of *Meditations for Troubled Marriages*, as well as numerous articles. She enjoys playing the piano and traveling. Freya and her husband have one son and make their home in New Brighton, Minn.

Dorothy M. Harpster is a retired elementary school teacher and the author of several devotions and articles. She enjoys writing, reading, and taking part in her church activities. Dorothy makes her home in Lewisburg, Pa.

L. Jane Johnson is a freelance writer who also enjoys reading and movie-watching. She makes her home in Boulder, Colo.

Debbie Kalmbach is a freelance writer and speaker. She is the author of *Corey's Dad Drinks Too Much* (Tyndale) and a contributing writer to devotional books and magazines. She enjoys hiking, cross-country skiing, cross-stitch, and playing the piano. She and her husband, Randy, have two sons and live in Auburn, Wash.

Nancy Kennedy is a freelance writer, string newspaper reporter, and author of a humorous take-off on the Proverbs 31 woman. She has contributed to numerous devotional books and magazines and enjoys T-shirt painting and working out at the gym. Nancy and her husband, Barry, have two daughters and live in Inverness, Fla.

Carla Anne Kirk works in sales and as a performing arts attendant. She enjoys writing, reading, and dance. In addition, she is working to get her certificate in ornamental plants (450 plants required). Carla and her husband, David, have three sons and reside in Wilmington, Del.

Berit Kjos is the author of *Under the Spell of Mother Earth*, *Your Child and New Age*, and *A Wardrobe from the King* (all by Victor) and numerous articles for national publications. She speaks on changes in education and spiritual transformation in America. Berit and her husband have three sons and live in Los Altos Hills, Calif.

Beverly LaHaye is the founder and director of Concerned Women for America. She is the co-author, with her husband, Dr. Tim LaHaye, of *The Act of Marriage* and the author of *The Spirit Controlled Woman*, *Who but a Woman*, and *The Desires of a Woman's Heart*.

Erma Landis is a homemaker and freelance writer of several articles. Erma enjoys reading and bird-watching. She has six married children and seventeen grandchildren and lives in Lititz, Pa.

Kathleen R. Lewis is a homemaker who enjoys reading, traveling, working with women's ministries in her church, and writing poetry. She and her husband have three grown daughters and three grandchildren and reside in San Rafael, Calif.

Linda Miller is a teacher and assistant director of special education for Dayton Christian School. She has published a spelling book for the Association of Christian Schools International. Her hobbies include writing and reading. Linda makes her home in Dayton, Ohio.

Shirley Mitchell is a homemaker, writer, and speaker. She has written two books for women in addition to a Christian Writer's Desk Diary. She is also a columnist for two weekly newspapers, writing "Fabulous After 50." Shirley and her husband, Jack, have three children and five granddaughters and live in Albertville, Ala.

Linda Montoya is a writer and speaker and works for Court Appointed Special Advocates. Her work has been published in numerous devotionals and magazines, including the Australian magazine, *The Encounter.* Linda and her husband, Frank, have three daughters and reside in Ventura, Calif.

Barbara L. Neiman has written numerous articles and poems. A freelance writer and speaker, she enjoys photography, needlepoint, camping, and traveling. She and her husband, Jim, have two grown sons and two grandchildren and make their home in Lynnwood, Wash.

Nancy Willis O'Meara is a physical therapist who enjoys writing, reading, and gardening. Nancy has written for the *Christian Medical/Dental Society Journal.* She and her husband, Clifton, have two children and reside in Georgetown, Tex.

Glenda Palmer is a homemaker and freelance writer who has written devotions, greeting cards, children's songs, and eight children's books. Her hobbies include reading, traveling, and camping. Glenda and her husband, Richard, have two grown sons and reside in El Cajon, Calif.

Aurora Presley is a full-time homemaker who enjoys writing, decorating, gardening, and painting. She and her husband, Gerry, have two sons and one daughter and make their home in Santa Rosa, Calif.

Mary Proctor is an accountant who is in the process of rewriting her company's accounting material. She is involved in her local church and enjoys portrait painting, sewing, bread-making, yard work, singing, and needlework. She has five grown children and resides in Raleigh, N. C.

Ruth M. Rink is a retired junior high school teacher who has written articles for her local newspaper and several devotions. Her hobbies include reading, journaling, and participating in discipleship and prayer groups. Ruth makes her home in Indiana, Pa.

Ruth Robinson-LaFreniere is a musician and speaker and former college professor and concert pianist. A hemiplegic, Ruth has learned to play piano with one hand and continues to give concerts and presentations nationwide. She and her husband, Paul, have six children and five grandchildren and reside in Salem, Ore.

Dorethea Schauber is a secretary who enjoys bowling, needlework, and walking. She has three daughters, three grandchildren, and one great-granddaughter. Dorethea makes her home in Winter Park, Fla.

Marilyn Zent Schlitz is in computer sales and enjoys teaching, writing, and painting. Marilyn has two grown daughters and two grown sons and resides in Tempe, Ariz.

Marcia Schwartz is an English and journalism teacher and author of several magazine articles. She enjoys reading, sewing, writing, photography, and "riding over the hills in our Jeep." She and her husband, Hank, have two grown sons and live in Falls City, Neb.

Sandy Sheppard is a freelance writer, homemaker, and former school teacher. She has authored several magazine articles and the book *Avaricious Aardvarks and Other Alphabet Tongue Twisters* (Standard). She enjoys reading and calligraphy. Sandy and her husband have three children and live in Cass City, Mich.

Janet Colsher Teitsort is an elementary school teacher and the author of several poems, devotions, and articles, as well as three books: *Rainbows for Teachers* and *Treasures for Teachers* (Baker), and *Quiet Times: Meditations for a Busy Woman* (Gibson). The Teitsorts have two children and four grandchildren and live in Westport, Ind.

Faye Hill Thompson is office manager of their family farm corporation and a former school teacher. In addition to writing, she enjoys reading, traveling, attending cultural

events, and co-teaching a high school Sunday School class. She and her husband, Noel, have one daughter and reside in Ellsworth, Iowa.

Doris Toppen has written a variety of magazine and newspaper articles and teaches creative writing classes through her community college. In addition to writing poetry, she enjoys biking, aerobics, gardening, camping, and reading. Doris has four grown children and five grandchildren and lives in North Bend, Wash.

Marcy Weydemuller is a homemaker who has written devotions and short stories and who enjoys reading, crocheting, Bible study, and teaching adult education classes at her church. She and her husband, Bob, have three children and make their home in Concord, Calif.

Jan Watrous Woodard has written over 450 articles and devotions. She is a freelance writer who hosts the radio interview program *Christian Witness*. A lay leader in her church, she and her husband have three children and live in Indiana, Pa.

Bobbie Yagel is a Bible teacher and speaker, and the author of two books, *Living with Yourself and Other Imperfect People* (Chosen) and *Building Better Relationships* (Aglow). Her hobbies include tennis and knitting. She and her husband, Myron, have three grown children and three grandchildren and live in Richmond, Va.

CREDITS

The following articles are used by permission of the publishers.

"God's in the Life-Changing Business!" by Annie Chapman was adapted from the book *The Strength of a Woman* edited by Linda McGinn, ©1993 Broadman & Holman Publishers, Nashville, Tenn. Used by permission.

"Pursuing a Disciplined Life" by Elisabeth Elliot was adapted from the book *Discipline, the Glad Surrender* by Elisabeth Elliot, © 1982 Elisabeth Elliot. Published by Fleming H. Revell, a division of Baker Book House Company, Grand Rapids, Mich. Used by permission.

"My First Priority in Life" by Ruth Bell Graham was adapted from the book *The Strength of a Woman* edited by Linda McGinn, ©1993 Broadman & Holman Publishers, Nashville, Tenn. Used by permission.

"From Fear to Faith" by Beverly LaHaye was adapted from the book *Prayer: God's Comfort for Today's Family* by Beverly La Haye.